2004

3 0301 00214779 7

John Paul II
& Educating for Life

PETER LANG
New York • Washington, D.C./Baltimore • Bern
Frankfurt am Main • Berlin • Brussels • Vienna • Oxford

James T. Byrnes

John Paul II
& Educating for Life

Moving Toward a Renewal
of Catholic Educational Philosophy

LIBRARY
UNIVERSITY OF ST. FRANCIS
JOLIET, ILLINOIS

PETER LANG
New York • Washington, D.C./Baltimore • Bern
Frankfurt am Main • Berlin • Brussels • Vienna • Oxford

Library of Congress Cataloging-in-Publication Data

Byrnes, James Thomas.
John Paul II and educating for life: moving toward a renewal
of Catholic educational philosophy / James T. Byrnes.
p. cm.
Includes bibliographical references (p.) and index.
1. John Paul II, Pope, 1920– —Views on education. 2. Catholic
Church—Education. 3. Educational change. I. Title.
LC485 .B97   371.071'2—dc21   2001037662
ISBN 0-8204-5703-5

Die Deutsche Bibliothek-CIP-Einheitsaufnahme

Byrnes, James T.:
John Paul II and educating for life: moving toward a renewal
of Catholic educational philosophy / James T. Byrnes.
–New York; Washington, D.C./Baltimore; Bern;
Frankfurt am Main; Berlin; Brussels; Vienna; Oxford: Lang.
ISBN 0-8204-5703-5

Cover design by Joni Holst

The paper in this book meets the guidelines for permanence and durability
of the Committee on Production Guidelines for Book Longevity
of the Council of Library Resources.

© 2002 Peter Lang Publishing, Inc., New York

All rights reserved.
Reprint or reproduction, even partially, in all forms such as microfilm,
xerography, microfiche, microcard, and offset strictly prohibited.

Printed in the United States of America

371.071
B995

12/31/03

This work is lovingly dedicated to my parents,

Edwin Joseph Byrnes and Mary Grace Norton Byrnes

whose self-giving love for each other formed the community into
which I was born and from which I have pursued my work of
self-education, transcendence, and self-fulfillment as a person.

TABLE OF CONTENTS

PREFACE

The original research for this work was begun when I was a graduate student at the Graduate School of Education of Fordham University in New York. Given my predilection for things philosophical and my work in Catholic education, it seemed only natural to me to pursue an investigation into Catholic educational philosophy. To my surprise—and chagrin—any serious work in this field, as I note later, seems to have ended in the early 1960s. Additionally, I found that the prevailing philosophical basis for most educational theorists (Catholic and non-Catholic alike) was some form of postmodernism.

What I found to be problematic, as a Catholic school educator, was accepting postmodernism as a philosophical basis for Catholic education. How was it possible to proclaim and teach Jesus as the Way, the Truth, and the Life, while accepting a philosophy which, for the most part, denies the reality of objective Truth and rejects the Christian metanarrative outright? To my mind, it was not possible, yet the educational *practices* being advocated by theorists who made postmodernism their own made tremendous sense. At this point that I came to see that there needed to be formulated a *via media*, which would incorporate much of the good in postmodern thought without sacrificing objective Truth and the Christian metanarrative. It is in the hope of beginning to map out this *via media* that I present the educational philosophy of John Paul II.

As will be seen, John Paul II (writing as Karol Wojtyla the philosopher) set out to construct a philosophy which would be a *via media* between Thomism and 20th Century philosophical thought. It is my belief that the greatest accomplishment of his thinking was the dialogue it encouraged amongst philosophers. I only hope that this presentation of his educational philosophy will encourage the same sort of dialogue among Catholic educators and that from this dialogue a new interest in articulating a Catholic philosophy of education will arise.

I would be remiss if I did not acknowledge some of those who helped bring the research I began 4 years ago to its present form. Firstly, I would like to thank Dr. John Elias of Fordham University for his guidance and his critiques of my work during our time together. He often brought order to chaos; his patience was heroic and his scholarship inspiring. Thanks also goes to Dr. Stephen Powers, whose wit made many hours of tedium much more endurable. My thanks, as well, to Rev. John M. Knapp who patiently listened to my many ramblings as the ideas in this work gradually took shape. Lastly, to His Eminence, John Cardinal O'Connor, the late Archbishop of New York, whose support and encouragement made this research possible—may he rest in peace.

I

A NEW APPRECIATION FOR
CATHOLIC EDUCATION

Education reform has been, and continues to be, an issue which is discussed and debated by all members of society, but receives the greatest attention from those holding public office and professional educators. It seems that all recognize that there is a problem with the education of our young people, especially when they are compared with the young people of many of the other industrialized nations throughout the world. There is little point to going through the litany of indicators which have brought so many voices together in calling for reform. Suffice it to say that there is a problem. The more difficult aspect of the reform movement in education is first identifying the problems and then coming to some agreement on how to proceed in order to bring about the needed changes.

An interesting result of all this debate has been a surge in the estimation of Catholic schools in the eyes of many people. Even ardent supporters of the public school system have been willing to admit that Catholic schools have done, and continue to do, an excellent job in educating the young people of our society, especially with those young people considered "at risk." From this rise in estimation has also come an attempt to discern what it is that Catholic schools are doing which could be used in the attempt to reform public education. The 1993 study by Bryk, Lee, & Holland, *Catholic Schools and the Common Good*, is one such attempt at identifying those factors which contribute to the high success rate of the Catholic school.

One need only to quickly peruse these factors to realize that they are not the *direct* result of religious beliefs or practices, but are rather the result of a *philosophical* view of the human person which is in complete harmony with the Catholic faith. This being the case, it is very possible to transpose many of the success factors of Catholic schools to their public counterparts without bringing with them the tenets of the Catholic faith. These factors would include (and this is not meant to be an exhaustive listing), respect for the dignity of each student, the need for community within the school, appreciation for the individual experiences of each member of the school community, and the unity of knowledge. What is amazing is the fact that many of the writers on educational reform have touched on one or all of these points in putting forward their ideas on the necessary reforms which should be implemented in schools throughout the country.

Obviously, in order to take up the above mentioned ideas and enable them to be implemented, these educational reform writers needed to ground them in a philosophical view of the human person. Since Modernism has been identified as the leading cause of the depersonalization and artificial division of knowledge in schools, these writers, for the most part, have come to embrace Postmodernism as the philosophical grounding of their reform goals. This has resulted in some fine efforts which, when one reads through them, should seem very familiar to Catholic school educators (one example being Patrick Slattery's *Curriculum Development in the Postmodern Era*, (1995).

The embracing of Postmodernism, however, was not without its negative aspects, at least from the Catholic perspective. One of the aspects referred to is the abandonment of the belief in an objective Truth, the search for which has been the goal of all education, and particularly Catholic education. Thus, it is possible to find a writer calling for respecting each person's opinion within the school—but this is done not because of the inherent dignity of the person, but rather because each opinion is equally valid, since truth is relative and determined by time, place and culture. Another negative aspect of Postmodernism is its rejection of metanarratives (i.e., universal explanations which claim to reveal truths), especially the Christian metanarrative which is often cited as the cause of many of humankinds problems. Even though these negative aspects are disconcerting, some comfort may be taken in the fact that, in many cases, the right thing is being done, albeit for the wrong reasons.

Catholic Education and the Reform Movement

While a new appreciation for Catholic education has been arising in those outside of Catholic education itself over the last number of years, there has been an effort on the part of Catholic educators themselves to examine their schools and continue to make changes in an effort to improve on their current success. This effort is not only laudable, but also necessary. Much has been written and work done to improve *how* things are done on all levels of Catholic education.

The area which recently (over the past 35 years) has not been given much attention, thought, and research, is understanding *why* Catholic schools operate as they do. Obviously, the teaching of Jesus can, and must, be the one source to which Catholic educators turn to understand the "why," and this has been spoken of (the United States Bishops' Conference's *To Teach as Jesus Did* is but one example). Jesus, however, did not give to his Church a blueprint to be followed in the conduct of the educational enterprise. From the earliest centuries of her existence, the Church has been involved in the work of education, and this vast amount of experience and reflection has produced an answer to why education is carried out in the way it is—a Catholic philosophy of education.

Up through the 1950's, it was possible to see numerous works (both books and articles) which discussed the philosophy of Catholic education with the early part of the 20th century being a particularly fruitful time. In the period since the Second Vatican Council, however, this is an area which has been largely abandoned. John Elias has presented a succinct explanation of why this occurred in his article, "Whatever happened to Catholic philosophy of education?" (1999).

The abandonment of the work of constructing a Catholic philosophy of education has left a vacuum which thereby left Catholic educators struggling to find a philosophical basis to support the work which they do so successfully. Unfortunately, since nature abhors a vacuum, Post-modernism has begun to be the philosophical base for many Catholic educators, which, although in actual educational practice may not be problematic, becomes problematic when faced with presenting the Christian metanarrative with Jesus as the Way, the Truth, and the Life.

Thus, a certain schizophrenia is detectable in many areas of Catholic education and among Catholic educators: on the one hand, significant agreement with the educational practices being proposed today and, on the other, disagreement with the rejection of the Gospel of Jesus. It is for this reason that Catholic educators must once again take up the task of renewing the rich heritage that is theirs in regard to a philosophy of education. This is not a call for a simple "return to what was," but rather a true dialogue with the present-day philosophical ideas, which will result in taking from both the old and the new.

It is to this end that this current work is directed. Selected writings of Pope John Paul II (Karol Wojtyla) will be examined and their application to education presented in order to provide Catholic school educators with an educational philosophy which, while remaining faithful to the philosophical tradition of the Church concerning education, acknowledges and incorporates the innovations in philosophical thought in the 20th century, especially phenomenology and existentialism. As will be mentioned later, John Paul II is in a unique position to discuss educational philosophy, since he himself spent many of his pre-papal years as a philosopher and, more importantly for our purposes, as a teacher.

The examination will focus primarily on four recurring philosophical themes in John Paul's pre-pontifical and pontifical writings (Person and Act, Community, Solidarity, and Participation) as well as his pontifical writings addressed specifically to youth. The philosophical themes and the writings to youth will be examined and their relationship to the educational process presented.

A Few Words Concerning Wojtyla's Writings

Analyzing the writing of a single author normally would not present any particular difficulties which need to be noted. This, however, is not the case with Wojtyla's works, as two specific issues arise given the significant change in his life when elected to the papacy in 1978. The first of these difficulties specifically concerns the change in roles which the papacy brought to him.

Before 1978, as priest, auxiliary bishop, and later as Archbishop of Krakow, Wojtyla wrote predominantly as a philosopher, who was able to bring a certain amount of speculation into his thought, because of his rather obscure position on the world stage. After becoming pope, Wojtyla had to take on the role of the authoritative teacher in all of his writings. This prevented him from employing the same type of speculative thought which one had been accustomed to when examining his pre-papal work. Wojtyla's role as authoritative teacher has effectively ended his ability to continue to write as a philosopher. Anyone attempting to present any aspect of Wojtyla's thought must deal with this issue. Rocco Buttiglione, a expositor of Wojtyla's philosophical thought, states that

> The criteria and the hermeneutical methods of philosophical thought differ from those which can be used to interpret the Pope's teaching, which have as their immediate antecedents not the thinking of the philosopher Wojtyla, but the acts of his predecessors and the entire Magisterium of the Church in its historical development. (1997, p. 306)

Buttiglione dealt with this issue by confining his investigation to Wojtyla's writings before becoming pope. Unfortunately, this investigation does not have the luxury of this option, since the vast majority of Wojtyla's writings dealing with education were written after he became pope. The need to draw upon both pre-papal and papal writings to present Wojtyla's philosophy of education makes it necessary to continually keep in mind which Wojtyla is writing, the philosopher or the pope. By so doing, it is possible to present a reasonable exposition of Wojtyla's educational philosophy.

The second area of difficulty encountered is, in a sense, another result of Wojtyla becoming pope in 1978. While most writers remain within the same milieu or genre for their entire writing careers, Wojtyla, once again, is an exception to this norm and thereby creates another methodological anomaly. The works which will be examined throughout this text are often amalgams of two distinct types of writing, philosophical and theological. Wojtyla, in his papal writings, skillfully moves between being the philosopher, the theologian and the authoritative teacher. Attempting to move back and forth between these genres and roles presented a challenge. The attempt to overcome this challenge unfortunately gives to some portions of this work a less than smooth transition between ideas in some sections.

Another methodological challenge presented by Wojtyla's election to the papacy is encountered in referencing authorship of Wojtyla's writings, given his name change to John Paul II after 16 October 1978. Throughout this text, the subject's given name, Karol Wojtyla, is used to refer to him both before and after he became pope. However, for clarity and exactness, any reference to his writings will make use of the papal name and/or the given surname. Thus, any work written prior to 16 October 1978 will be referenced, both in the text and the reference section, as "Wojtyla" while any work written after this date will be referenced as "Wojtyla/John Paul II." It is hoped that this form of referencing will aid the reader in noting the philosophical-theological and philosopher-authoritative teacher distinctions.

Arrangement of the Work

Chapter II will examine the development of a Catholic philosophy of education during the 20th century, especially the contributions of Jacques

Maritain and personalism. The point is made that throughout the course of this century, the Church has continued to reflect upon the education of young people as conceived within a philosophical understanding of the human person and society. While the first half of this century was marked by a certain mistrust and wariness regarding new secular philosophical and educational thought, the latter part has been marked by a desire to incorporate the best of the old with the best of the new.

This chapter also provides an overview of the various writings of Karol Wojtyla which will be examined throughout the book. The presentation is divided into his pre-pontifical and pontifical works which should be helpful in better understanding the context in which Wojtyla wrote.

Chapter III seeks to explore Wojtyla's idea of the human person through a detailed presentation of his main philosophical themes. This is accomplished primarily by examining his central philosophical text, *The Acting Person* (Wojtyla, 1979a). It is in understanding how he views the individual person that insight can be reached as to the purpose of education and the pedagogical methods used in schools. Also found in this chapter is a brief analysis of Wojtyla's understanding of the relationship between faith and reason, and how this relationship impacts upon the educative process. The presentation of his main philosophical themes helps the reader to understand the significance of Wojtyla's thought upon education. This chapter also seeks to place Wojtyla within the context of 20th century philosophical thought while at the same time acknowledging his ties to more "traditional" philosophical systems by presenting a brief biography and noting his philosophical forebears. The chapter concludes with a critical analysis of Wojtyla's thought in the light of modernism and deconstructive postmodernism.

In Chapter IV, Wojtyla's understanding of the human person is placed within the context of education. Central to this chapter are the concepts of freedom, personal responsibility, self education, and self-fulfillment. It is in this chapter that the teacher's role in the educative process is taken up as well as the teacher's personal relationship with Jesus Christ.

Chapter V examines the role of community in the education of the young person. The importance of the school as a Christian community is taken up as well as the importance of giving of self to the community. Also, a presentation of the entire issue of participation is given. It is in the discussion concerning participation (and its antithesis, alienation), that the reader will be able to discern the influence of Marxist philosophy upon the personalist school of thought. Flowing from this is an examination of Wojtyla's concept of solidarity and how it relates to education. There is little doubt that solidarity is central to Wojtyla's presentation of the Gospel and his discussion of human rights. Solidarity also speaks to those involved in education; both in regard to the secular sciences as well as to the faith.

Chapter VI concerns itself with Wojtyla's understanding of what it means to be a young person, and how this understanding can help to guide those involved with the education of young persons. As was mentioned above, Wojtyla has the utmost regard for the young people of the world and has sought to provide them with an understanding of their state in life. Chapter VI has a different approach then the previous chapters, since here is found Wojtyla speaking as a pastor to the young people in his charge. The material presented is from Wojtyla's homilies and letters to young people. While not philosophical in nature, these writings are critical to understanding Wojtyla's philosophy of education since they show how he himself would put his educational philosophy into action. In this chapter as well is a discussion on the role of the student in the educative process. Of importance here is the concept that it is in Jesus Christ alone that the young person will find his or her true human personhood. Jesus alone is the answer to the searchings of the young human heart.

The final chapter, Chapter VII, presents a summary of Wojtyla's philosophy of education in the form of the "dream school" Wojtyla would establish. Presented here, as well, are the significance of Wojtyla's thought in terms of the actual praxis of Catholic education, his place in the development of a Catholic philosophy of education and some closing reflections.

II

CATHOLIC PHILOSOPHY OF EDUCATION
IN CONTEXT

Since the first days of apostolic preaching, the Church has been involved in education, both religious and secular. The history of this involvement, while of interest, is much too lengthy and intricate to be related here. What is of importance to this study is the state of Catholic thought and intellectual life in the 20th century and how this affected the articulation of a distinctly Catholic philosophy of education. Throughout the 20th century, there has been a reasonably healthy tension within the Church between traditional and innovative philosophical (theological) thought. This tension was often played out between the Church hierarchy and theologians as both attempted to bring the faith to the world using concepts and terminology that today's person would understand.

The beginning of the century was marked by a reluctance, on the part of the hierarchy, to allow philosophical and or theological thought to incorporate the best of modern thinking as it could be applied to education, and, for that matter, all aspects of the Church's life and belief. This was done in an effort to protect the faith from those elements of modern thought which threatened to undermine belief. Truly, the Second Vatican Council was the watershed; the hierarchy strove to open the Church to that which was good in modern thought (the Council documents themselves reflect, in the terminology and approach used, this acceptance of modern thought). Many of the philosophers and theologians who, before the Council, were considered to be "suspect" in their thinking, were the very ones to whom the Council turned to clarify and explain the faith.

Examining this somewhat turbulent period, from the point of view of Catholic education, is essential in order to appreciate the importance of the work of Karol Wojtyla in the ongoing task of articulating a Catholic philosophy of education for the 21st century. Wojtyla himself was, as a young bishop at the Second Vatican Council, one of the leading proponents of bringing to the traditional teachings of the Church the insights which modern thought presented (Kwitny, 1997, pp. 187–189). It will be seen that all of Wojtyla's thought is an attempt to continue this effort begun so many years before. With this in mind, it is possible and necessary to briefly examine the Church's understanding of Catholic education in the 20th century.

Reaction to the Enlightenment

From the foundation of the first European universities until the close of the 19th century, Catholic educational philosophy (indeed, all Catholic teaching) had rested securely upon Scholastic thought, particularly that of Thomas Aquinas. Spurred on by the "siege mentality" of the Counter-Reformation, the Church saw no need to engage Enlightenment thinkers in debate nor was it thought that these thinkers had anything to add to the work of the Angelic Doctor, as Aquinas was referred to, or to the Divine Revelation of which the Church was custodian. It was only after observing the major social and intellectual changes of the later 19th century that some Catholic intellectuals began to look toward some aspects of Enlightenment thought for answers.

Aside from being the pope who ushered in the 20th century, (being pope from 1878 until his death in 1903), Leo XIII also distinguished himself by his attempt to respond "officially" to the societal and intellectual "upheavals" of his day, which were brought about by Enlightenment and Marxist philosophers. This response took the form, for the most part, of encyclicals and apostolic letters, one of which is pertinent to the present discussion: *Aeterni Patris*. Written in 1879, *Aeterni Patris* was a call from the pope to Catholic intellectuals (both theological and philosophical) to return to the thought of Thomas Aquinas in order to respond to the errors of Enlightenment and Marxist thought. Leo's attempt did bring about a "rediscovery" of Thomistic thought (now known as Neo-Thomism) which was to serve as a means of articulating a Catholic philosophy of education between the World Wars, as shall be seen. Although heeded by many, Leo's call did not stem the enthusiasm of some within the Church for "new" philosophical approaches to be accepted.

In the closing days of his pontificate, Leo was faced with the need to respond to Enlightenment and Marxist thought in a more aggressive manner, by making use of official condemnation and excommunication. Both in the United States and in Europe, Catholic intellectuals were ordered to recant many of the philosophical ideas of the Enlightenment which they had come to espouse. The condemnation of Americanism (in the papal letter *Testem Benevolentiae*) and Modernism (in the encyclical, *Pacendi* of Leo's successor Pius X), as these errors were entitled in the United States and Europe, respectively, took a heavy toll on Catholic thought. In *Contending with Modernity*, Philip Gleason notes,

> *Testem Benevolentiae's* chilling effect on Catholic intellectual life was heavily reinforced by the condemnation of Modernism in the next decade. Modernism, which was primarily a European phenomenon, brought on a much more serious crisis for the Church as a whole, but it resembled Americanism in that it too resulted from efforts to synthesize the Catholic faith with contemporary modes of thought and the results of modern scholarship. (1995, p. 12)

The harm to Catholic intellectual life arose mainly from the "witch hunt" mentality which followed the condemnations. Catholic thinkers were wary of being involved in any discussions or proposals which might hint at being "modernistic." This resulted in many giving up any attempt to engage the secular thinkers of their day in conversation.

While the debate will go on concerning the validity of the condemnation of Americanism and Modernism and the nature of the harm caused to Catholic intellectual life, one fact is undeniable: Leo's call for a renewed examination of Thomism sowed seeds which would have a profound effect on Catholic educational philosophy in the 20th century.

The next event of interest to this brief overview occurred some 30 years after Leo's death. In 1929, Pope Pius XI issued *Divini Illius Magistri*, the only papal encyclical to deal *directly* with Catholic education (others, such as Wojtyla's *Catechesi Tradendae*, deal with religious formation, not pedagogy). *Divini Illius Magistri* can properly be seen as a continued response, on the part of the Church, to the Enlightenment since it offered a critique of the new "progressive" education. The "progressive" educators offered a view of the human person which was opposed to much of the Scriptures and Church dogma but, for the most part, in harmony with Enlightenment thought. As Elias notes,

> The encyclical did two main things: it made the case for the teaching mission of the Church and for traditional Catholic education, and it attacked certain aspects of progressive education. Its main quarrel with progressive education was the latter's rejection of the overriding importance of religion in education and its denial of the doctrine of original sin. (1997)

Although the encyclical was defensive of traditional teaching of the Church, it did provide a starting point for the construction of a true Catholic philosophy of education which would be built upon "officially" by the Second Vatican Council as well as the Congregation for Education, in the years following the Council.

Personalism

The seeds sown by Leo XIII in *Aeterni Patris* began to sprout and flourish, in Europe during the period between the World Wars, as Neo-Thomism. It was during this time that the personalist school of thought arose. Being Neo-Thomistic in nature, it sought to bring to Thomas' thought a new approach which would be relevant to 20th century humankind while at the same time be in concert with traditional Catholic philosophical thought. It should be noted that many of the members of this school of thought were actively engaged in education as teachers. Since Wojtyla is clearly within this school of thought philosophically (Doran, 1996, pp. 25-27), the importance of personalism to any discussion of Catholic philosophy of education cannot be over empha-sized and a presentation of its basic thought is necessary.

Although mainly of French origins, Emmanuel Mounier (with the journal, *Esprit*) and Jacques Maritain being its more well known adherents, personalism did have its proponents in other parts of Europe and the United States and was not limited to Catholic, or even Christian, sensibilities.

> Most of the earliest and most important articulations of personalism were by German-educated, militantly anticommunist Russians, Germans, and Belgians, who were Russian Orthodox, Jewish, or non-believers. Despite the pre-eminence of Mounier, personalism was hardly a French Catholic creation. There was... 'something German and Jewish about it,' and the defense of the person...was rooted in Bergson and Nietzsche more than the gospels. (Hellman, 1981, p. 5)

The fact that it could not be attributed to one particular ethnic or religious group is what enabled personalism to become so popular.

Personalism, is, when all is said and done, a philosophy which sees each human person as a unique individual who is at once both spiritual and physical (body and soul). It arose as a reaction to both the inhumanity experienced by Western civilization during World War I as well as the

Modern era's philosophical depersonalization and emphasis on conscious-ness. Mounier is careful to point out that to speak of a purely "spiritual" or purely "physical" issue in a person is impossible since every real activity of the person involves the material and the spiritual. He writes,

> My moods and my ideas are shaped by the climate, by geography, by my situation upon the crust of the earth, by my heredity and perhaps beyond all this by unfathomable currents of cosmic rays. Into these influences the supervening psychological and collective determinants are interwoven; there is nothing in me that is not mingled with the earth and the blood. (Mounier, 1970, p. 3)

Because of this intrinsic union of body and soul, the human person possesses an incomparable dignity which must always be respected.

Personalism, however, does not extol the individual human person at the expense of others. It is important to note that personalism is *not* the same as subjective individualism (which is inherently self-centered) nor is it the narcissism of the "me" cult (Buetow, 1988). Personalism "consists in the insight that we are creatures of freedom, by which we shape our own destiny. Our nature is determined by relationship to others, and is fulfilled by the gift of self in love" (Caldecott, 1992, p. 272). Human nature is, therefore, essentially relational. In order to fulfill what it means to be "person" (in the philosophical sense) we must be involved in a community of others and live out our lives in that community by the constant gift of self.

Although personalism does see community and communication with others as the pathway for fully actualizing the person, it must also be noted that this position does not place the community above the individual. In all cases, the dignity and importance of the individual must be respected, and changes made in the community if there is a demeaning of the person. The community is the means to personal fulfillment and is therefore important but should never be seen as the greater end of the person. Although personalist thinkers put forward much the same critique of society as the Marxists (adopting much of the same terminology as Marx), their overall view of the human person prevented them from ever seeing the person as subservient to the state. It is for this reason that the personalists were vehemently opposed to the totalitarian regimes, whether Fascist or Communist, which were arising throughout Europe.

Personalism and Education

The representative of the personalist school of thought who was to bring personalism to education was Jacques Maritain. Although it appears that Maritain's influence on Wojtyla's thought was less than that of Mounier's (Doran, 1996), he still occupies an important place in the development of a Catholic philosophy of education in the 20th century. The place he occupies becomes even more evident when considering the influence he had upon various bishops during the Second Vatican Council (Wojtyla, included) as well as on Pope Paul VI.

Although Maritain, as a personalist, clearly exalts the wonder and dignity of the human person, he does not advocate the individualism of the Enlightenment philosophers which removed any sense of a shared human experience and knowledge. It is this understanding that he is able to bring to the developing Catholic philosophy of education. From the personalist perspective (following Aristotelian and Thomistic thought) it is the spiritual superexistence of each person which unites all human persons as members of the same species. It is only when we communicate and share our spiritual selves with another that we can be known and understood as a person. In other words, if we seek to express our uniqueness as persons by "doing our own thing" or "whatever we feel like," we are not expressing ourselves as a person, but as one whose personhood is dominated by one's physical nature, not one's spiritual superexistence. Maritain explains this concept by speaking of the tension between *individuality* and *personality* within the person:

> Personality means interiority to oneself; this internal selfhood grows in proportion as the life of reason and freedom dominates over the life of instinct and sensual desire—which implies self-sacrifice, striving toward self-perfection and love. But individuality, in the strict Aristotelian sense in which I am using the word...means the material ego, the displaying of which consists in giving a free hand to the irrational trends of this ego. (1943, p. 34)

It is possible to understand and know another person when each person is able to establish commonality of expression with each other and this commonality is found in the spiritual self. This commonality allowed Maritain to speak of education serving the truth; there is an objective truth which the person must search for.

Maritain views human beings as persons who are in control of their own destiny as lived out in community (society). Human persons act in freedom when they exercise their respective *personalities* in order to give of themselves to the community. The community (made up of other persons) in turn, gives to other persons the ability to freely fulfill their *personalities*. What we see in Maritain is, therefore, a realization that the person has intrinsic dignity and is unique, but this same person must act within community (society) in order to realize his full potential. The rugged individualism of the Enlightenment is replaced by the notion of person-in-community. Maritain writes,

> Thus it is that social life tends to emancipate man from the bondage of material nature. It subordinates the individual to the common good, but always in order that the common good flow back upon the individuals, and that they enjoy that freedom of expansion or independence which is insured by the economic guarantees of labor and ownership, political rights, civil virtues, and the cultivation of the mind. (1943, p.14)

What Maritain and personalism are able to bring to the traditional Thomistic view of the person is the concept of social justice. By so doing, he is able to present personalism as an alternative to Marxism; one need not embrace Marxist ideology to enter the discussion regarding human rights and societal justice.

It is from this background that Maritain presents a personalistic view of education in the first sentences of *Education at the Crossroads*. He writes, "Thus the chief task of education is above all to shape man, or to guide the evolving dynamism through which man forms himself as a man" (Maritain, 1943, p. 1).

The "evolving dynamism" of which Maritain speaks is the intellect of the person. As we have seen above, the intellect forms the centerpiece of the spiritual superexistence which maintains the personhood of the individual. Thus, the intellect must be cared for and helped to develop properly if the human being is to be able to come to achieve his or her full potential as a person. Education is the process by which the intellect of the person is awakened to its full potential through the guidance of the educator. For Maritain, then, the student is the principal actor in the process of education and the teacher's role is secondary: it is the students who, with proper guidance, are to achieve their full intellectual potential. He writes,

> All this boils down to the fact that the mind's natural activity on the part of the learner and the intellectual guidance on the part of the teacher are both dynamic

factors in education, but that the principal agent in education, the primary dynamic factor or propelling force, is the internal vital principle in the one to be educated; the educator or teacher is only the secondary - though a genuinely effective—dynamic factor and ministerial agent. (Maritain, 1943, p. 31)

Maritain sees that, through education, the mind of the young person should be guided by the teacher so as to arrive at the stage of development where thinking and a constant intellectual desire for discovering the truth (objective truth) becomes second nature (Maritain, 1943, p. 26).

When this stage is reached, the person has achieved true freedom of thought and has brought to consciousness the natural God-given activity of intellect which separates the human person from the animal world. By quickening the intellect, the person is indeed educated and then able to master the sense information which is apprehended. The educated person is, therefore, a person whose intellect is able to analyze information, draw conclusions, and make generalizations. With this ability, the person is then well equipped to take on any challenge of life or any chosen occupation because the person can *think*. Quite literally, education is the awakening of a process, not an imparting of information. After this process is brought to the fore, the intellect seeks after and can and should comprehend information on its own (Maritain, 1943, p. 50).

Although this brief presentation cannot do justice to Maritain's philosophy of education, it is possible to note that even in the personalist Maritain there is still a very strong sense of the Scholastic. Education is seen as a function of the intellect and its ultimate purpose is to properly form the intellect of the person. The educative process is reducible, therefore, to intellectual functioning. While Maritain added much to a developing Catholic philosophy of education for the 20th century, its strong Scholastic character resulted in its being abandoned by many involved in Catholic education, especially after the Second Vatican Council. A fuller philosophy was desired, one which was able to borrow from insights into human existence made by 20th century philosophical thinking.

It is interesting to note that personalist thought is still very prevalent in the praxis (if not the philosophy) of Catholic educators today. Concerning Catholic schools where student success is high, Bryk, Lee, and Holland have noted that,

Teachers are firm and committed to high standards in classroom work, but they simultaneously display a strong personal interest in students, both in and outside the classroom. Both their language and behavior bespeak a strong sense of commitment to individual students and to a school life permeated with Christian Personalism. (Bryk, Lee, & Holland, 1993, pp. 94-95)

Personalism will continue to be a part of any articulation of a Catholic philosophy of education.

The Second Vatican Council and the Congregation for Education

The Second Vatican Council was convened by Pope John XXIII in 1961 in an attempt to give to the Church an *aggiornamento*, an "opening of the windows" of the Church's life to the modern world. What was desired by John XXIII and many other bishops who attended the Council was a dialogue between the Church and modern thought. In a sense, the "siege mentality" was to be replaced by an acceptance of that which was good in current (or modern) scholarship and praxis. The Council sought to enter into the dialogue as an equal; a partner in the quest for the truth, not the dispenser of all truth. It is important to realize that the Council understood that the Church had much to offer to secular society, while at the same time she could learn as well.

The Council also contributed to the continuing understanding of Catholic education in its Decree on Christian Education, *Gravissimum Educationis,* issued at the close of the Council in 1965. This decree provides a synthesis of traditional teaching regarding education (as presented by Pius XI in *Divini Illius Magistri*) and personalism. The decree also encouraged Catholic educators to continue to take that which is good from new secular educational philosophy and theory while maintaining the truths of Divine Revelation concerning the human person.

Following the lead of the Council, the Congregation for Catholic Education has issued three documents, *The Catholic School* in 1977, *The Religious Dimension of Education in a Catholic School* in 1988, and *The Catholic School on the Threshold of the Third Millenium* in 1997. These documents emphasize the need for Catholic schools to make use of the best in secular educational theory as they proceed with the task of educating young people as well as the role of the teacher in this task. These documents were not issued as Catholic philosophies of education; it is possible, however, to note similarities in thought to the personalist philosophy of education as found in the work of Maritain.

As was indicated in the preceding paragraph, the major documents issued regarding education from the time of the Second Vatican Council onward do not attempt to present a Catholic philosophy of education. They present methods and ideas regarding education, but not a philosophy as such. It seems that the continuing work of developing a Catholic philosophy of education ended sometime during the 1950s, at approximately the same time neo-Thomism, as a philosophical school of thought, fell out of favor (Elias, 1999, p. 94). The causes for this are numerous, but Elias has attributed this decline to "changes within the Catholic Church and within the general field of philosophy of education" (1999, p. 101), changes which have led to a move away from metaphysics as a valid starting point for philosophical inquiry.

Because Wojtyla maintains a metaphysical starting point, his writing can be one avenue by which to, once again, take up the work of formulating a Catholic philosophy of education flowing from the rich tradition of neo-Thomism from the earlier years of the 20th century.

Wojtyla's Personalism and Education

Karol Wojtyla, especially after his becoming Pope John Paul II, has made young people an important part of his ministry. His interest in their education and full development as human persons is evident in the many allocutions and letters presented to them. Throughout all of these opportunities to speak with young people, he is strong in his affirmation of much of what modern society has to offer while at the same time equally strong in his conviction that only in Jesus Christ can a person be fully human. He continues the effort, which he began so clearly at the Second Vatican Council, to bring the best of modern thought into dialogue with the truth of the message of Jesus.

In addition to his direct work with young people, Wojtyla often meets with educators on the primary, secondary, and university levels. During these meetings, he has consistently reminded educators of their responsibility to become aware of and utilize new pedagogical methods and educational theory in their work with students. He has also recognized the need for new methods to be in concert with the professed aims of Catholic education. Addressing Catholic schoolteachers gathered in New Orleans in 1987 he stated that there is, in Catholic education, the pressing challenge of clearly identifying the aims of Catholic education and applying proper methods in Catholic elementary and secondary education and religious education programs. It is the challenge of fully understanding the educational enterprise, of properly evaluating its content and of transmitting the full truth concerning the human person, created in God's image and called to life in Christ through the Holy Spirit. (Wojtyla/John Paul II, 1987b, p. 154)

Wojtyla's comments clearly indicate his awareness of the value of many new and, in some cases, rediscovered, methods and theories regarding school culture and pedagogical methods which have been presented in recent years.

Karol Wojtyla's philosophical understanding of human persons is in many ways reminiscent of the thought of Thomas Aquinas. At the same time, he has brought to this "traditional" philosophy new insights taken from phenomenology and existentialism. As Schmitz has noted, "Wojtyla is confident that modern techniques and approaches, and above all phenomenology properly modified, can help us to explore the inner region of human experience. But these techniques must first be purged of their idealism and subjectivism and be brought into harmony with a realistic metaphysics" (1993, p. 38). This "new" approach takes into account so much of what has been learned regarding the inadequacy of modernism as a way of life for the 21ˢᵗ century. What results is a philosophy which can provide a theoretical base for a Catholic philosophy of education for the 21ˢᵗ century while at the same time remaining in harmony with the Christian gospel taught and proclaimed in the Catholic school as well as neo-Thomistic personalism .

This being said, it must also be noted that Wojtyla remains very securely within the framework of Catholic educational thought which has been outlined above. While seeking to bring certain new philosophical approaches to educational thought, many of his ideas reflect the educational ideas first presented by Pius XI (1929) in *Divini Illius Magistri* and developed in the decrees of the Second Vatican Council.

The Writings of Karol Wojtyla

Before beginning to organize the basic lines of Wojtyla's thought regarding education, it is important to understand the breadth and diversity of the writings which he produced over the past 55 years. Ranging from the theoretical to the hortatory and the philosophical to the spiritual, the sum Wojtyla's works provide an insight into the philosopher, the educator and the pope. The brief overview that follows provides only an introduction to his works relating to education—the real merit of Wojtyla's thought is its coherence of philosophical and theological ideas.

Pre-Pontifical Works. Karol Wojtyla, aside from being the first non-Italian pope in 450 years, occupies a unique position among his 20th century papal predecessors. This uniqueness stems from the fact that Wojtyla spent much of his pre-pontifical life as a philosopher and university professor (continuing in these roles even while Archbishop of Krakow). Given this background, there is a large corpus of Wojtyla's writings available, and these writings provide the philosophical basis to all his thought.

Additionally, because of Wojtyla's continuing interaction with university students, many of the works speak of the intellectual and spiritual development of the young person. This interest in the full development of the young person continued after he became pope as evidenced by the extensive corpus of writings addressed specifically to young persons as well as his bi-annual gathering with young people from all over the world (the various World Youth Days).

In 1960, shortly after becoming Archbishop of Krakow, Wojtyla wrote the first of his major works, *Love and Responsibility* (Wojtyla, 1981). This work, written as a guide to help young people prepare for marriage, presents, in germinal form, Wojtyla's metaphysical understanding of the human person. The text is eminently readable and is important to this study because it presents the significance of personal self-fulfillment in developing interpersonal relationships. Additionally, *Love and Responsibility* introduces the concept of solidarity (which is a central idea in many of his later writings), as well as self-education and personal responsibility. Solidarity implies that persons work together, as equals, toward an agreed upon common good. When solidarity is present, persons are treated as subjects called to be in communion with rather than objects to be used. This study will make use of these concepts as they apply to education and leadership in schools.

The Acting Person (Wojtyla, 1979a), is the centerpiece of Wojtyla's philosophical thought. It presents an understanding of the human person which is based upon traditional Thomistic thought into which are integrated various insights developed from the use of phenomenological methodology of investigation. Written in 1969 and originally published in Polish as *Osoba i czyn* (Person and Act), the work is woefully lacking in concrete examples, which would have served to elucidate Wojtyla's main points. Although the work is dense and often obscure, it does enable the reader to grasp Wojtyla's fundamental view of the human person, which is imperative to fully understand all his other works. Other concepts presented in *The Acting Person* include how a person comes to have knowledge, community, participation, alienation, solidarity, and truth (in both its objective and subjective sense). All of these concepts will provide important data in the formulation of Wojtyla's philosophy of education.

From 1962 until 1965, Wojtyla was an active participant in the Second Vatican Council (Vatican II). Upon his return from Rome to Krakow, he began the process of implementing the reforms of the Council within his Archdiocese. He provided a text to introduce the faithful to the teachings of Vatican II by giving his reflections on the Council documents. This work, *Sources of Renewal: The Implementation of Vatican II* (Wojtyla, 1980), provides important insights into the themes of participation, community, solidarity, and freedom, all of which Wojtyla saw as present in the documents of Vatican II. Additionally, it is interesting to note that Wojtyla's official "interventions" during the Council itself all related to these themes (Schmitz, 1993, appendix); there is no mistake as to the influence which Wojtyla had at Vatican II. As mentioned above, these particular themes are of great importance in drawing together Wojtyla's educational philosophy.

In more recent years, many of Wojtyla's essays and lectures have been collected and translated for the English speaking world. *Person and Community: Selected Essays* (Wojtyla, 1993) is one such text. As the title of the collection implies, a major theme of the essays is how the individual person relates to the community. Here, again, are found the ideas of participation, alienation, and community. In addition, Wojtyla reflects upon the meaning of self-determination and culture. All of these concepts contribute to his understanding of the educative process.

Another area touched upon in this collection of essays is the family, which is, for Wojtyla, the foundation for community and education of the child. Seeing the family as the primary site for the education of the young person is in no way revolutionary; it has been the theme of almost all Church teaching regarding education from *Divini Illius Magistri* (Pius XI,

1929) to the present. What begins to take shape in Wojtyla's work is how the family (specifically, though not exclusively, parents) brings about this education. This point will be of importance to consider in this text since the school has always been presented, by the magisterial documents of the Church, as standing in the place of the parent.

An aspect of Karol Wojtyla's unique background is the fact that he spent a good portion of his youth in the theatre as an actor and playwright. He actually contemplated a career as an actor, but gave up that vocation when he felt called to the priesthood. Because of this background, one is able to gain much insight into Wojtyla's thought through his theatrical and poetic writings. *The Collected Plays and Writings on Theater* (Wojtyla, 1987) and *The Place Within: The Poetry of Pope John Paul II* (Wojtyla, 1997a) are two texts which are useful in fully appreciating and understanding Wojtyla's ideas. The concept which is most striking in these texts is the importance of personal experience in the life of the person (this emphasis on experience has persuaded many to view Wojtyla as a phenomenologist). The idea of personal experience is important for understanding much of what Wojtyla writes regarding the development (education) of the young person.

Pontifical Works. On 16 October 1978, Karol Wojtyla was elected to the papacy. As John Paul II, he has traveled more widely and has directly addressed more young people than any Pope in history. Given his desire to consistently engage young people (which he does with charismatic effectiveness), it is not surprising that great insight can be gained about Wojtyla's overall philosophy of education by examining his written and spoken words since becoming Pope. Also worth noting is the continuity of thought and expression from his earlier works, mentioned above, to his more recent papal writings and allocutions.

On 16 October 1979, one year after becoming Pope, Wojtyla issued the first of his major documents, *Catechesi Tradendae* (Wojtyla/John Paul II, 1979b). This document was his own synthesis of the work of the 1977 Synod of Bishops which discussed the topic of catechesis. Although the document speaks about the education of the person in the faith, it does give the reader some insights into Wojtyla's ideas regarding education in general. Present throughout *Catechesi Tradendae* are the many themes already highlighted from Wojtyla's pre-pontifical writings. Often, there is reason to question the authorship of documents issued by the popes; in this case (as is true for all the documents and allocutions which will be cited herein) there is little doubt as to the authorship. The themes and style too clearly reflect the mind of Wojtyla to have been penned by anyone else, even a close friend and confidant. *Catechesi Tradendae* is also important to the construction of Wojtyla's philosophy of education because it presents the role of faith in all aspects of the educational process.

Another of Wojtyla's specifically educational writings is *Ex Corde Ecclesiae* (Wojtyla/John Paul II, 1990a) in which he addressed the role and nature of the Catholic university. Here, again, many of the same themes are present as were found in his other works. Specifically mentioned are the importance of community, the nature of truth, the solidarity of all and the place the university has in influencing culture. *Ex Corde Ecclesiae* and *Catechesi Tradendae* form Wojtyla's only lengthy expositions regarding education; other works containing references to education are either much shorter allocutions or lengthier texts on another topic.

In 1985, Wojtyla wrote *To the Youth of the World* (Wojtyla/John Paul II, 1985) to mark the occasion of the United Nations' International Youth Year. This letter explores what occurs in the development of the person while he or she is young. An important idea emanating from this is the concept of self-fulfillment which is discussed at length by Wojtyla in *The Acting Person* (Wojtyla, 1979a). This "self-fulfillment" plays an important part in Wojtyla's philosophy of education because it is, for him, a hallmark of the human person. Additionally, many of these themes, as well as issues of spiritual development and education can be found in Wojtyla's messages for the annual World Youth Days.

Because of the family's role in forming the larger community of society, Wojtyla has written extensively on the family both before and after he became pope. Two of his pontifical works, *Familiaris Consortio* (Wojtyla/John Paul II, 1981) and *Letter to Families* (Wojtyla/John Paul II, 1994c), are of particular note. Both of these texts contain some discussion on the role the family plays in the education of children. This role is especially important to consider in this study since the school is often called upon to become the "family" for many young people in modern society. Here again are found the familiar themes mentioned above.

In September of 1987, Wojtyla made another pastoral visit to the United States. During his visit to New Orleans, Louisiana, he had the opportunity to speak to Catholic schoolteachers, Catholic university professors and administrators, and young people. The content of all of these allocutions provide more insight into Wojtyla's thought on education. Particularly evident was the emphasis on the importance of community in the school. These allocutions (Wojtyla/John Paul II, 1987b) provide a clear integration of Wojtyla's philosophical anthropology with the work of education and are therefore significant primary sources for this study, even though they are not scholarly treatises.

In 1994, Wojtyla gave an interview to Vittorio Messori which eventually became the work *Crossing the Threshold of Hope* (Wojtyla/John Paul II, 1994c). This text provides an opportunity to hear an older Wojtyla speak on a variety of issues. Of interest is the section of the book in which Wojtyla gives some reflection on young people: their natural gifts, curiosity, and wants, what they have to offer to the world. While the themes are not new, it is important to note how optimistic the 79-year-old Wojtyla remained in regard to the young people of the world. There is also a clear mention of how the older generation can be of assistance to the maturing and development of the young person.

One of Wojtyla's more recent lengthy works is the encyclical letter *Fides et Ratio* (Wojtyla/John Paul II, 1998a). This encyclical presents in very clear fashion not only the integral relationship between faith and reason, but also the importance of a solid philosophical background for religious belief and human knowledge. Coupled with *Veritatis Splendor* (Wojtyla/John Paul II, 1994a), this encyclical provides important background in that Wojtyla's metaphysical presuppositions, especially regarding the nature and validity of objective truth, are succinctly presented. While neither of these encyclicals represent new ideas on Wojtyla's part, they do provide a fine synthesis of his thought and therefore will be of assistance to anyone seeking to apprehend his philosophy of education. Additionally, these two works bring to the fore various concepts which impact substantially on the praxis of education, both secular and religious.

III

THE PERSON IN THE PHILOSOPHY OF KAROL WOJTYLA

Indeed, experience is that specific form of the actualization of the human subject which man owes to consciousness. Because of it the actual "energies" which we discover through action in man as a type of being are actualized according to the pattern of subjectiveness proper to man as a person. Moreover, while so actualized they receive in experience their final, so to say, subjective shape. (Wojtyla, 1979a, pp. 46–47)

The above quote, taken from *The Acting Person*, provides an insight into the importance of life experience in a person's ability to fully apprehend the world around him. While this understanding carries important ramifications for the education of the person, which will be discussed later, it is introduced here to provide the reader with the rationale underlying the content presented in this chapter.

Because individual experience clearly takes on, in Wojtyla's thought, a formative role in the human person's understanding of the objective world, any person seeking to draw forth his philosophy of education must have a working knowledge of Wojtyla's own experiences. With this in mind, the first section of this chapter will present a brief biography of Karol Wojtyla. This biography, while being in no way exhaustive, will provide the reader with a view of the life experiences which helped to shape Karol Wojtyla the person, and therefore his philosophy. Additionally, this biography will serve as a means to present, at least in chronological order, those philosophers whose thoughts helped shape Wojtyla's own philosophical anthropology.

The second section of this chapter, as the title indicates, will be a presentation of Wojtyla's philosophy of the human person. It would clearly be impossible to construct or comprehend Wojtyla's thinking on education without coming to terms with his basic vision of the human person and the individual person's place in society, as well as the person's relationship with God. Here, again, Wojtyla's understanding of the

LIBRARY
UNIVERSITY OF ST. FRANCIS
JOLIET, ILLINOIS

importance and role of experience in the life of the individual person will be evident.

With the road to be traveled within this chapter thus plotted out, it is now possible to begin the journey by turning attention to Wojtyla's life and to those who influenced his thought.

Karol Wojtyla's Early Life and Influences

Karol Wojtyla was born on 18 May 1920 in the small town of Wadowice, which is located in the mountainous region of southwest Poland, near the Austrian border. Wojtyla's father, Karol senior, was a lieutenant in the Polish army, attaining this position after the creation of modern Poland at the conclusion of World War I. His mother, Emilia Kaczorowska Wojtyla, was the daughter of a middle class family. Karol senior and Emilia were married in 1904, to the consternation of the Kaczorowska family who believed their daughter was marrying beneath her social class (Kwitny, 1997).

The two settled in Wadowice following their marriage and lived a relatively peaceful, if not poor, life, and having three children: Edmund (born 1906), a daughter who died at birth (in 1914) and Karol junior. Edmund, being significantly older than his younger brother, was away from the family home through all of Karol junior's younger school years, being first at the Jagiellonian University and then the medical school of this same institution. The Wojtyla's family life was happy and religious though always overshadowed by Emilia's chronic illness, of which there is no definite description, which led to her untimely death on 13 April 1929 (Kwitny, 1997, p. 34). The death of his mother deeply affected the younger Karol, and his experience of being motherless led him to a deep devotion to the Blessed Virgin Mary, a devotion which continues to play an important role in his piety (O'Brien, 1998, p. 87).

When Edmund finished his medical studies in 1930, Karol senior and junior were in attendance at his graduation in Krakow. Edmund's studies now completed, he took a position on the staff of a hospital much closer to Wadowice which allowed the Wojtyla brothers to renew their relationship. From all accounts, the two were together as often as Edmund's schedule would allow (Kwitny, 1997, p. 37). This renewed closeness made Edmund's sudden death in 1932 (from scarlet fever, contracted from his patients during an epidemic) all the more traumatic for the young Karol. Reflecting on his brother's death after becoming pope, Wojtyla noted, "my mother's death made a deep impression...and my brother's perhaps a still deeper one because of the dramatic circumstances in which it occurred and because I was more mature. Thus quite soon I became a motherless only child" (Frossard, 1984, p. 14).

Although there was much sadness which both Karols had to endure, Karol junior's life and relationship with his father was, by all descriptions, loving and normal (Kwitny, 1997, p. 36 and O'Brien, 1998, pp. 77–80). Additionally, the experience of watching how his father dealt with tragedy and suffering clearly had an impact on him. Concerning his father, Wojtyla noted that

> almost all my memories of childhood and adolescence are connected with my father. The violence of the blows that struck him opened up immense spiritual depths in him; his grief found its outlet in prayer. The mere fact of seeing him on his knees had a decisive influence on my early years. He was so hard on himself that he had no need to be hard on his son; his example alone was sufficient to inculcate discipline and a sense of duty. (Frossard, 1984, p. 14)

Karol junior's life outside the home in Wadowice was typical of any schoolboy of his day. He was always a good student, but was no academic recluse, being involved with his parish, both as an altarboy and leader of the Sodality of the Blessed Virgin, and always counted on to be a part of the soccer games played by the boys after school. For all the normalcy of his grammar and high school years, those who knew Wojtyla well in those days always note that he was different, in the good sense of the word. They note that he possessed,

> a humor that was so subtle that it was difficult to define – an affectionate sort of irony that endeared him to others less studious and religious than he. There was a reserve about him that commanded respect, yet he was also curious about others...Talking to him gave the impression that he knew what you were saying better than you did yourself. (O'Brien, 1998, p. 78)

These qualities made him a popular young man and also one with innate leadership abilities.

While Wadowice seemed to be, on first observation, a typical Polish village of its day, it did have one characteristic that set it apart from the vast majority of other towns and cities in Poland during the late 1920s and 1930s. This characteristic was the absence of abject anti-Semitism. The good relations between Catholics and Jews seemed to have been fostered by Canon Prochownik, the parish priest of Wadowice, who made it very clear to his congregation that anti-Semitism had no place in the mind or heart of a Catholic Christian (Weigel, 1999, p. 39). This teaching was not lost on young Wojtyla, who developed a close and lasting friendship with Jerzy Kluger, one of his Jewish Wadowice classmates. Wojtyla would also play the position of goalie for his Jewish classmates whenever the after-school soccer teams were divided along religious lines (O'Brien, 1998, pp. 52-54).

These experiences of the attitude toward Judaism of Canon Prochownik, and Wojtyla's own friendship with Jews during his school years, taught the young Wojtyla to disregard and disavow anti-Semitic propaganda which flourished around him. As O'Brien (1998) notes, concerning the importance of these personal experiences, "Wojtyla's friendship with one Jew...in Wadowice is a significant factor in understanding his character. As with all his ideas, his understanding of Jews and Judaism came not from received opinion or doctrine but out of personal experience that was later shaped by religious and philosophical tradition" (p. 96). Because O'Brien's text concerns itself with the friend-ship between Wojtyla and Jerzy Kluger, and not Wojtyla's philosophical ideas, the above quote is all the more significant. From early on, Wojtyla appears to have been coming to appreciate the role of personal experience in both his own education and its role in understanding the human person.

As he continued through high school, Wojtyla was becoming more and more involved with another activity, the experience of which would also have a significant influence on his life. This activity was the theater and the person behind it was Dr. Mieczyslaw Kotlarczyk. During these years, Wojtyla performed in no fewer than eight plays, sometimes playing double roles when other actors were ill (Kwitny, p. 46). His interest in the theater was encouraged by Dr. Kotlarczyk, his Polish teacher, with whom he would later work as a university student. These experiences on stage served to direct Wojtyla to both his university major (Polish philology) and, as he believed at the time, his vocation (an actor). Boleslaw Taborski, the translator of Wojtyla's theatrical writings, has noted that Wojtyla's abilities on stage were remarkable, not only for his ability to memorize the lines of all the characters, but also for the quality of his performance (Taborski, 1987, p. 2).

Wojtyla concluded his high school years in June of 1938 and was graduated as valedictorian. His academic career had been exemplary, languages being his strong suit and he was prepared to begin classes at the Jagiellonian University in Krakow the following September. Even at this early stage in his life, Wojtyla's innate abilities were recognized. Adam Sapieha, the archbishop of Krakow, was in attendance at the high school graduation and heard Wojtyla deliver his valedictory address. Sapieha asked the parish priest if the young Wojtyla was going to pursue theology at the university, obviously hoping the priesthood was a possibility. When told that Wojtyla intended to study literature and become an actor, Sapieha responded "that's a pity" (Kwitny, p. 49). Coming from Sapieha, who was well educated himself and from a Polish noble family, this statement was high praise indeed. Wojtyla would not have, at this time, ever imagined that Sapieha would be ordaining him to the priesthood in just six short years nor would he have guessed the many experiences which these succeeding six years would bring.

In August of 1938, the two Wojtylas moved from Wadowice to the first floor of a house in Krakow, so as to remain together while Karol junior was attending the university. This residence was shared by the remaining members of Emilia Wojtyla's family; Karol junior had inherited a share in the house from his mother at her death. The animosity from Emilia's family towards her marriage must have continued, because there appears to have been very little interaction between the Wojtylas and the rest of the family (Kwitny, 1997, p. 50). Although small and cramped, even for only two people, the residence was located conveniently to both the University and the Wawel Cathedral, the two places which were central to the lives of both father and son.

During his first year of university study, Wojtyla took courses which clearly underscored his intent to pursue a career on the stage. Additionally, and perhaps most importantly to his mind, he became involved in a student theater group and began to associate with the members of the group on a social level as well. The members of this group remember him in much the same way his high school acquaintances did: friendly but reserved, academically serious, and a fine actor. As he continued with his studies, he also began to write his own poetry as well, most of which was very reflective and often difficult to understand. This first year seemed a very happy and productive time for Wojtyla; he was able to be involved in both study and his first love, the theater.

Unfortunately for him, and the rest of the Polish people, this period of contentment was soon to come to an abrupt halt.

On 1 September, 1939, as Wojtyla was serving early morning mass in the cathedral, as was his custom, the Nazi blitzkrieg began. Within two weeks, all of Poland was occupied by the advancing Nazis or the Soviets who chose to take their share of the prize (Kwitny, 1997, pp. 54–56). Krakow was located in the middle of the Nazi zone and soon all sense of normalcy was gone. The university was closed and many of the professors were transported to internment camps in various parts of the Third Reich. Also outlawed were the many amateur theater groups which had been so prevalent (Kwitny, 1997, p. 57).

In a few short days, the life Wojtyla had come to know so well was shattered and necessity caused him to rearrange his entire life. Although the university was officially closed, groups of students would meet with the remaining professors for some semblance of a class. Clearly, anyone participating in these classes would have been arrested or executed if caught, but Wojtyla and many other students believed that the opportunity was worth the risk. Along with the underground university classes, underground theater groups arose as well which performed in "safe" apartments for small audiences. The plays performed were, most often, works from the neo-romantic period of Polish literature; plays which spoke of the destiny of Poland to overthrow their oppressors. While the themes of these plays could not have been more appropriate for the overrun Poles, they were clearly anathema to the Nazis. The members of these theater groups were therefore in constant danger of arrest or deportation to concentration camps (Kwitny, 1997, p. 58).

Wojtyla had begun a life fraught with danger and yet one which he believed to be worth the danger. It is also during this period that the experiences which would be so influential and formative of Wojtyla's later thought occur and his vocation to the priesthood would become apparent. So apparent, in fact, that he would enter the underground seminary being run by Archbishop Sapieha; the same person who noted his talents only a few years before.

The first of these experiences which would prove to be so formative is the meeting of Wojtyla and Jan Tyranowski. Tyranowski, a layman, was something of a mystic and sought to encourage university students to be apostles to their peers by means of small "Living Rosary" groups. He was a devotee of the Carmelite mystics, Saints Teresa of Avila and John of the

Cross, and possessed a full understanding of their works, as well as practical experience with their spirituality. He had the reputation of being an eccentric, albeit holy man (Malinski, 1979, p. 20). Although he was not officially a minister of the Church, Tyranowski's influence on the young people he singled out was significant, life-long, and well respected. He was clearly responsible for numerous vocations to the priesthood.

Wojtyla's introduction to Tyranowski was accidental, to be sure. Because the Wawel Cathedral was closed by the Nazis, Wojtyla began attending daily mass at the nearest parish Church. It was after mass one day that Wojtyla was approached by Tyranowski and asked to join a "Living Rosary" group. Both men would often meet and it was during these meetings that Tyranowski gradually introduced the young Wojtyla to mystical theology and meditation in the Carmelite tradition. From Tyranowski, Wojtyla received his appreciation for Saint John of the Cross, whose work inspired his first doctoral dissertation. Additionally, Tyranowski's connection with the Catholic Action movement (Malinski, 1979, p. 18), may also have provided Wojtyla with an introduction to the thought of Emmanuel Mounier, a connection of which more will be said later. The influence of Tyranowski upon Wojtyla cannot be overemphasized and it is clear that this influence helped to shape his philosophical thinking, as well as his vocation to the priesthood and spiritual life.

Although Wojtyla was involved in many activities during Nazi occupation, the underground classes and theatrical productions had to wait until the evening. During the day he was obliged to work. When the Nazi's occupied Krakow, they decreed that all males between the ages of 14 and 60 must work at some legitimate job or face deportment to concentration camps. Wojtyla first found work as a waiter but then, luckily, he was able to work at a factory which produced items necessary for the war effort. This job afforded Wojtyla the added advantage of receiving identity papers which effectively made him immune to deportment; his work was indispensable (Malinski, 1979, p. 64).

The experience of physical labor and the camaraderie of his fellow workers gave rise to many thoughts in Wojtyla's sharp mind. These thoughts found release in the poetry he wrote describing his experiences (Wojtyla, 1997a, pp. 63–71). What appears to have influenced Wojtyla the most was the realization that the human person is more than just a cog in the machine of factory or state. This realization also helped to shape his views of both communism and materialistic capitalism. He writes,

> Hands are the heart's landscape. They split sometimes
> Like ravines into which an undefined force rolls.
> The very same hands which man only opens
> When his palms have had their fill of toil.
> Now he sees: because of him alone can others walk in peace...
> No, not just hands drooping with the hammer's weight,
> Not the taut torso, muscles shaping their own style,
> But thought informing his work...
>
> So for a moment he is a Gothic building
> Cut by a vertical thought born in the eyes.
> No, not a profile alone,
> Not a mere figure between God and the stone,
> Sentenced to grandeur and error. (Wojtyla, 1997a, pp. 64-65)

What is seen in these words of the twenty year old Wojtyla are themes which will become the centerpiece of his philosophical thought: the dignity of the human person as well as the revelatory and personal nature of the human act. More will be said concerning these ideas below.

From almost the time the Wojtylas' arrived in Krakow, Karol senior had not been well. When the first of the Nazi bombs began to fall in September of 1939, Karol junior had to beg a place on a truck leaving Krakow for the safety of the surrounding countryside, because his father was unable to walk the few miles (O'Brien, 1998, p. 175). By the winter of 1941, the elder Wojtyla was bedridden. On his way home from his job, Karol junior would stop at the home of his close friends the Kydrynskis, to pick up the evening meal which he and his father would share in their own home (Kwitny, 1997, p. 70).

On the evening of 18 February, 1941, after picking up his father's medication and their evening meal at the Kydrynskis', Karol walked to his home in the company of Maria, the Kydrynskis' daughter. Arriving at home, Karol found his father "sprawled on the bed, dead, his legs over the edge, as if he had been trying to get up when a stroke or heart attack felled him" (Kwitny, 1997, p. 70). The fact that his father had died without him being present upset him all the more because all of his loved ones had died without him being at their side. He eventually came to the painful realization that all those whom he loved were gone from his life by the time he was 20 years of age.

After adjusting to his loss, Wojtyla came to see that being alone did give him the freedom to make choices in his life without the responsibility of caring for his family. Some saw it in terms of divine destiny (Kwitny, 1997, p. 70). The themes of freedom and responsibility in the life of the human person are ones which will be seen throughout Wojtyla's philosophical writings. The experience of the death of his father seemed to bring them to the fore in his own life so that they were not just abstract concepts to him.

Another experience which served to influence the thinking of Wojtyla during this time was his involvement in the formation of the Rhapsodic Theater group. Soon after the Nazi push through Poland on the way to the Russian Front, Wojtyla's former high school teacher and theatrical mentor, Dr. Mieczyslaw Kotlarczyk arrived in Krakow with his family. He and his family left Wadowice when the Nazis advanced because he was one of the few intellectuals left there; he was very correctly concerned that he would be a target for deportation. Since Wojtyla's father had just died, Karol offered the relocated family space in his own tiny apartment (Kwitny, 1997, p. 71). Wojtyla and Kotlarczyk had maintained correspondence from the time the Wojtylas left Wadowice for Krakow. Wojtyla often wrote to his friend and mentor describing the plays he was writing and asking for advice on his acting career.

Soon after the Kotlarczyk's arrival in Krakow, he and Wojtyla began an underground theater group. The two gave it the name Rhapsodic Theater; it was to be a "theater of the word" in which the lines spoken by the actors conveyed all the meaning. There was to be only minimal scenery and props, since the dialogue had to bring the entire message which the playwright wished to convey. Obviously, this minimalistic approach to theater lent itself well to the war time situation in which the actors found themselves. This, however, was not the impetus behind the work of either Wojtyla or Kotlarczyk: they sought to bring the word to each person and allow that person to take from this word the meaning the particular situation indicated. As Taborski explains, in speaking about Rhapsodic Theater productions,

> Kotlarczyk and Wojtyla were determined to rediscover the true meanings of the masterpieces of national literature...The carefully constructed scenarios, the equally careful choice of texts, the strict adherence to the adopted acting

convention, the use of props, and so forth made for a ritualized theater par
excellence. It was a kind of ritual the audience could share, a religious and
national ritual heightened in its significance by the situation in which the
participants and spectators found themselves. (Taborski, 1987, p. 7)

Wojtyla's theatrical technique shows an approach which will become
important in his later philosophical writings: the need to take into account
the subjective experience of the person when attempting to understand an
objective concept or truth. More will be said regarding this below.

The many events which surrounded Wojtyla during those first years of
Nazi occupation had profound effects, some of which have been noted
above. The most decisive effect was that Wojtyla came to the realization
that he had a vocation to the priesthood. Reflecting on these events later in
his life, Wojtyla seems to still be in awe of the change which had come
about in his life. "After my father's death, I gradually became aware of my
true path. I was working at the factory and devoting myself, as far as the
terrors of the occupation allowed, to my taste for literature and drama. My
priestly vocation took shape in the midst of all that. I knew that I was
called" (Frossard, 1984, p. 15).

In the first days of November, 1942, Wojtyla went to the Archbishop's
residence next to the Wawel Cathedral. There he was interviewed by
Archbishop Sapieha and asked to be admitted to the underground
seminary. Sapieha granted his request and Wojtyla became part of a very
small and clandestine group of young men. Because of the continued
dangers of the Nazi occupation, the seminarians continued with their day
jobs and met with their professors in the evenings or during other spare
moments. All were keenly aware of the dangers they faced if they were
discovered studying for the priesthood; for this reason it was a topic never
discussed with anyone outside of the group (Malinski, 1979, p. 47).

Even with his keen mind, Wojtyla's first foray into philosophy did not
come easily. He was given a book on metaphysics and found it nearly
incomprehensible at the beginning. One of his seminary classmates from
this time, Mieczyslaw Malinski, recalls the conversation he had with
Wojtyla concerning the text.

One day we were walking...and I asked him what book he had under his arm.
He showed it to me, but I had never heard of the author or the title. 'Are you
reading this?' 'Yes, but it's hard going. I sit beside the boiler and try to
understand it—I feel it ought to be important to me.' Next time we met I asked
him how he was getting on with the book, and he expressed discouragement.

Later, however, he came to admire it more and more, and said it had opened up a new world to him. (Malinski, 1979, pp. 47-48)

Although he had a difficult beginning as a philosopher, Wojtyla quickly adjusted himself to his philosophical studies and found in them an interest which would last throughout his life.

It was during his seminary studies in philosophy that he began to assimilate those philosophical positions which he would later develop as his own in *The Acting Person*. The three philosophers whose works were a major influence on Wojtyla's thought in these early years and, indeed, throughout his entire life, were (are) Thomas Aquinas, Max Scheler, and Emmanuel Mounier. Regarding the influence of Aquinas and Scheler, Wojtyla states, in the introduction to *The Acting Person*, that, "The author of the present study owes everything to the systems of metaphysics, of anthropology, and of Aristotelian-Thomistic ethics on the one hand, and to phenomenology, above all in Scheler's interpretation...on the other hand" (Wojtyla, 1979a, p. xiv).

Wojtyla is indebted to Max Scheler most specifically for introducing him to the phenomenological method of philosophical inquiry which Wojtyla makes use of in his seminal philosophical work, *The Acting Person*. Wojtyla studied Scheler in depth and produced the dissertation, *On the Possibility of Constructing a Christian Ethic on the Basis of the System of Max Scheler* (Wojtyla, 1959), in order to obtain his second doctorate. How Wojtyla first came in contact with Max Scheler's work is somewhat unclear, although the connection may well have come through Edith Stein, another philosophical disciple of Husserl who later became a Carmelite nun. Wojtyla's interest in the Carmelites may have led him to Stein's work and from there to Scheler's (Buttiglione, 1997, p. 54). Regardless of how he came to know of Scheler, Wojtyla spent much time and effort in coming to understand Scheler's work. In order to fully appreciate Wojtyla's methodology which he adopted from Scheler, one must have a cursory understanding of who Max Scheler is and his relationship with phenomenology.

Scheler was, at the outset of his philosophical studies, a disciple of Edmund Husserl, the founder of phenomenology. He eventually moved away from his master when Husserl, in his later years, moved toward Idealism (Buttiglione, 1997, p. 55). Although he rejected Husserl's turn toward Idealism, Scheler still remained convinced of the value of the phenomenological method of inquiry in order to investigate reality.

Scheler had an interest in ethics, especially the work of Immanuel Kant, and made use of phenomenological methodology to further his study in this area. Scheler did convert to Catholicism at the age of fourteen, because of his delight in the ceremonies of the Church, although he eventually did leave the Church toward the end of his life, seemingly due to his dislike for its moral teachings (Kwitny, 1997, p. 129). It appears that it was both Scheler's interest in ethics and the phenomenological method which he used to study ethics which interested Wojtyla. Although finally concluding that Scheler's ethical system could not be used to construct a Christian ethical structure, Wojtyla took from his study of Scheler the phenomenological method of investigation which he would use in all his own work.

Although Wojtyla himself does not directly mention the influence of Mounier on his work, Kevin Doran has made a convincing case for this influence. Doran writes, "Karol Wojtyla does not acknowledge the influence of Emmanuel Mounier in the way that he acknowledges that of Max Scheler or of St. Thomas. There is ample evidence, however, both historically and in the writings of Wojtyla, to make a case for this influence" (1996, p. 25). There is no need to present Doran's case in its entirety here, but his text certainly leaves one with the opinion that Mounier's influence on Wojtyla cannot be reasonably called into question. One need only casually read through Mounier's *Personalism* to see the emergence of the same themes which will be taken up by Wojtyla such as community, freedom and responsibility, transcendence, and the personal act. Wojtyla will add to and elaborate on these areas in his own work, but the overall connection is clear. A detailed analysis of Mounier's specific contributions to Wojtyla is not possible here. Suffice it to say that just as Wojtyla obtained his philosophical method of inquiry from the work of Max Scheler, a significant portion of his metaphysical grounding was obtained from Mounier.

Another influence, which Wojtyla himself has acknowledged, came from "the philosophers of dialogue, such as Martin Buber" (Wojtyla/John Paul II, 1994c, p. 36). These philosophers spoke, as did Aquinas, of the human being's nature being communal; human beings need to be in relation with one another. This concept, both for Aquinas and Buber, flowed from their belief in the revelation of God to humanity through the Bible. Wojtyla writes,

> Where did the philosophers of dialogue learn this? Foremost, they learned it from their experience of the Bible. In the sphere of the everyday, man's entire life is one of "co-existence"—"thou" and "I"—and also in the sphere of the absolute and definitive: "I" and "THOU." The biblical tradition revolves around this "THOU," who is first the God of Abraham, Isaac, and Jacob, the God of the Fathers, and then the God of Jesus Christ and the apostles, the God of our faith. (Wojtyla, 1994c, p. 36)

Buber's influence, as well as that of the Scriptures, can be most clearly seen in Wojtyla's thought regarding community and horizontal transcendence, concepts to be elaborated upon below. Wojtyla also looks to Buber and the other "philosophers of dialogue" not just in regard to the relationship between the "I" and "Thou," but also in their work to return to a true philosophy of being through "an integral metaphysics" (Wojtyla/ John Paul II, 1994c, p. 35). It is this return to an integral metaphysics which will set Wojtyla at odds with current postmodern deconstructionism, as shall be discussed later in this chapter.

While there is ample evidence to suggest that Wojtyla's familiarity with these above mentioned philosophers began during his seminary days because of the prevailing philosophical trends in Polish universities of the day (Doran, 1996 and Seifert, 1981), it would be incorrect to conclude that the development of his philosophical thought ended in 1946, with his ordination to the priesthood. Wojtyla's academic ability was recognized by his seminary professors from the start. One in particular, Father Rozycki, his professor of dogmatic theology, suggested that he begin work on a doctoral thesis. Because of Wojtyla's continued interest in the Carmelite mystics, Rozycki suggested he take as a theme, "The theological virtue of faith in Saint John of the Cross" (Malinski, 1979, pp. 88–89). This suggestion seemed to sit well with Wojtyla, given his wide range of reading of the works of the Carmelite mystic since they were first introduced to him by Jan Tyranowski at the beginning of the war.

Clearly, it was not just Wojtyla's seminary professors who saw his academic potential. Archbishop Sapieha, who had just arrived back in Krakow from Rome after receiving the Cardinals' "red hat," chose Wojtyla and Staszek Starowieyski, another seminarian, to go to Rome to pursue doctoral degrees at the Pontifical University of Saint Thomas Aquinas. Although there is speculation that Wojtyla was sent only to "accompany" Starowieyski, who was from a noble family and seemed to be "bishop material" (Kwitny, 1997, p. 95), it is likely that, with Wojtyla's abilities,

Sapieha would have sent him anyway. Wojtyla, it seems, was destined for a career as an academic; to be a university professor who would help rebuild the faculty at the Jagiellonian which had been decimated by Nazi atrocities during the Occupation. That he would be an academic was true, that he would be only an academic was another issue.

Having examined those experiences and persons which influenced Wojtyla's thought during his university and seminary days, it is now possible to look at his work at the Pontifical University of Saint Thomas Aquinas, in Rome, in the years following his ordination to the priesthood. It is during these years that his own philosophy of the person began to form and solidify.

Wojtyla's Life as Priest and Bishop

The Pontifical University of Saint Thomas Aquinas, or the Angelicum, as it is more commonly known, is conducted by the Dominican Order, of which Aquinas is still the intellectual shining star. Not surprisingly, the Angelicum was, when Wojtyla studied there, a stronghold for Thomistic thought. Representing traditional Thomism was Reginald Garrigou-Lagrange, who had been on the faculty of the Angelicum since 1909, and it seems that Wojtyla was pulled in the general direction of this traditional understanding of St. Thomas (Kwitny, 1997, p. 99).

Since Wojtyla had not had a systematic philosophical training in Krakow, his advisor thought it best for him to "first ground himself in basics by writing a preliminary paper on the theology of Thomas" (Kwitny, 1997, p. 99). This he did and received a perfect score from the three professors on his review panel (one of whom was Garrigou-Lagrange). Following this successful work, Wojtyla began work on his dissertation, the title of which he had received from his seminary professor when in Krakow: *Faith According to Saint John of the Cross* (Wojtyla, 1981d). This work was an attempt to speak about the importance of the human will in the search for God. This confronted the prevailing idea (in traditional Thomism) that this search was carried out by the human intellect rather than the human will. It was in this attempt that Wojtyla first embarked upon his philosophical odyssey seeking to bring together traditional Thomistic metaphysics with an understanding that the actions of the human person are more than simply actions of the person's intellect. This work also indicated that Wojtyla, although always remaining a Thomist, was not going to remain completely within the framework of traditional Thomism. His move toward personalism, as propounded by Emmanuel Mounier, had begun.

Wojtyla defended his dissertation in the spring of 1948, and returned to Krakow by the beginning of the summer. Although his formal studies were completed, Wojtyla would continue to hone his philosophical skills while a parish priest and an university professor.

Upon his return to Krakow, Cardinal Sapieha appointed the 27 year old Wojtyla as a curate of a small country parish in the town of Niegowic. While some saw this is a sign of disfavor, those who understood Sapieha knew that just the opposite was the case. Wojtyla had been assigned to a small parish, but the pastor of this parish was looked upon as one of the finest priests of the Archdiocese of Krakow; clearly Sapieha wanted the best possible start for the new priest in whom much had been invested (Malinski, 1979, p. 94). While in this, his first parish, Wojtyla began to learn the practicalities of being a parish priest. Additionally, he continued his reading in philosophy and pursued those philosophical interests which had been peaked during his time in Rome. His interest in becoming more proficient in philosophy was spurred on by his distress over the fact that the philosophy department at the Jagiellonian, his alma mater, had become predominantly Marxist. Given the expectation that he would soon be a professor in that very department, Wojtyla knew that he needed to be very well versed in all aspects of current philosophical thought. When asked, during his time at Niegowic, what academic writing and research he was engaged in, Wojtyla replied,

> I write various articles, but what seems to me most important at the moment is to reconcile Thomist philosophy with that of Max Scheler, who of course was Husserl's disciple. I am fascinated by Scheler's theory of values and of human nature. Phenomenology seems to me a fine philosophical instrument, but no more than that. It lacks a general world-view, a metaphysic if you like, and it would be worth while to create one. (Malinski, 1979, p. 113)

This quote sums up precisely what would become the main effort of Wojtyla's philosophical investigations: using phenomenological methodology to arrive at a fuller understanding of the human person as presented by Thomistic metaphysics. His attempt at accomplishing this task would eventually become his central philosophical work, *The Acting Person* (Wojtyla, 1979a).

In March of 1949, after less than a year in Niegowic, Sapieha appointed Wojtyla as a curate at Saint Florian's, a large parish in the heart of the old city of Krakow. This parish had the added advantage of being only minutes from the entrance to the Jagiellonian University, as well as a focal point for the university's students and faculty (Kwitny, 1997, p. 114). It was during this time that Wojtyla began working in earnest with young people, an effort which he would continue all his life, even as pope. His efforts were not aimed at providing recreational activities, although even these had a place, but rather at helping the young people to understand who they were and what they could be. This idea continues to play a part in Wojtyla's thought and is also a component of his understanding of education.

In September of 1951, Wojtyla left parish ministry and once again became a full time academician. He was asked by Sapieha to write a "habilitation" dissertation concerning Max Scheler's philosophy as a basis for Christian ethics. The dissertation, *On the Possibility of Constructing a Christian Ethic on the Basis of the System of Max Scheler* (Wojtyla, 1959), gave Wojtyla his second doctorate as well as the right to be a professor at the Jagiellonian University, which granted him the degree. Wojtyla was a popular professor and was often sought out by his students for advice on religious and personal problems, as well as for assistance in their course work (Malinski, 1979, pp. 108–110). All during this time he continued to write extensively; scholarly articles, theological texts as well as poetry and drama were all areas to which he set his hand. By this time of his life, his philosophical ideas were in place, although the ideas would continue to be refined as he was called upon to lecture and write more detailed articles. His central work, *The Acting Person*, would not be completed until 1969, some years after he had left his philosophical mark on the Second Vatican Council and had become the cardinal-archbishop of Krakow.

This brief look at Wojtyla's life ends here. While many of the written works which will be used in this study of Wojtyla's philosophy of education were composed after he became pope in 1978, the main purpose of this section has been accomplished: those philosophers and events which provided the background and influences for Wojtyla's philosophy of the human person have been examined. What must also be kept in mind is that this philosopher is also a man of faith and that

Wojtyla's firm faith, in the Catholic tradition, has played an important role in the development of his philosophical thought.

As will be seen, the philosophy of the person which Wojtyla developed is continually relied upon in his pastoral, spiritual, and theological writings as archbishop and pope. Although the philosophical approach of Wojtyla is evident in his papal writings, it is important to realize that, in his ministry as pope, Wojtyla's ability to be the speculative philosopher is greatly diminished. As pope, he writes and speaks as the head of the Magisterium, and as such does not venture into areas which would correctly be termed philosophical speculation. Buttiglione notes this point in his introduction to the third Polish edition of Wojtyla's *The Acting Person* (Buttiglione, 1997, p. 353).

Having seen, however cursorily, the influences upon Wojtyla as he developed his philosophy of the person, it is now possible to turn to the task of presenting this philosophy.

Karol Wojtyla's Philosophy of the Person

The hallmark of Wojtyla's philosophy of the human person is the emphasis which he places upon the uniqueness and value of each individual person. This emphasis, while being a central teaching of Christianity, finds its roots in Wojtyla's philosophical work. *The Acting Person* is presented by him as a work of philosophy: his conclusions concerning the dignity of the human person arise from the philosophical investigations carried out. In other works as well, Wojtyla's defense of the dignity of the human person is a clear indication of his personalist background. He is always careful to maintain the delicate balance between the individual person and the community, an activity common to all personalist philosophers, but especially Mounier. Concerning community and the human person Wojtyla writes, "How easy it is to think and judge on the basis of people en masse. And yet we must transvalue every numerical aggregate of people according to the principle of the person and the dignity of the person" (Wojtyla, 1993, p. 179).

There can be little doubt, as well, that this emphasis arose, not just from his personalist philosophical background, but also from the depersonalization he witnessed under both Nazi Occupation and Communism, once again underscoring the importance of personal experience in Wojtyla's philosophical work.

His seminary classmate and early biographer, Mieczyslaw Malinski, presents a fine summary of Wojtyla's methodology which is worth quoting at length as an introduction to Wojtyla's philosophy of the Person. Malinski writes,

> I saw the effect of the work he had been doing on Max Scheler's philosophy: a new way of thinking and of observing humanity...Karol was not concerned merely with emotions and experiences but with the whole of human personality, including will and intellect as well as feeling...Listening to him I realized more and more clearly that the field of experience on which all his abstract thinking was based consisted in his day-to-day contacts with all manner of people, and especially the young folk...With his penetrating mind he strove to observe and analyze human behaviour and so arrive at a synthetic conception of humanity. (Malinski, 1979, pp. 137-138)

Wojtyla maintains that traditional metaphysics failed to take the entire being of the human person into account when presenting a philosophy of the person. He remedies this in his own work by using human experience as his starting point and constructing his philosophy of the person based upon this.

It is important to realize that Wojtyla is not seeking to present a reconstructed version of Thomistic metaphysics. He is seeking to examine what it means to be a person using phenomenological methods. Buttiglione (1997) notes that, "For Wojtyla, it is not a question of demonstrating phenomenologically that man is a person, but seeing with the aid of phenomenology *in what way man is a person*, in which way the metaphysical structures proper to his being are reflected in his consciousness" (p. 356).

Although Wojtyla arrives at many of the same conclusions put forward by Thomistic metaphysics through this process of phenomenological inquiry, he believes his methodology frees his metaphysics from many of the criticisms of Thomas Aquinas put forward by post-scholastic philosophers. There are those who would not so readily agree with Wojtyla's assessment of his own work and therefore the concluding pages of this chapter will examine some critiques of Wojtyla's methodology and overall philosophy.

The "I" Presupposes Being. The first, and most basic, point made by Wojtyla is that there is a need to return philosophical inquiry to its grounding in reality, as was found in the Scholastic tradition. He offers a basic critique that most philosophy since Descartes has turned in on the self, making subjectivity, self-consciousness, and self-reflection the reality of the person. That is to say, consciousness or self-reflection constitutes the person. This was done in reaction to the Scholastics who tended to under-emphasize the subjective. Wojtyla's position, which he comes to through his phenomenological methodology, is that while consciousness is important when discussing the person, it is the *person* who is conscious or self-reflective; the person must first exist in order to be conscious. He writes that in post-Cartesian thought,

> the aspect of consciousness eventually assumed a kind of absolutization, which in the contemporary era entered phenomenology by way of Husserl. The gnosiological attitude in philosophy has replaced the metaphysical attitude...The reality of the person, however, demands the restoration of the notion of conscious being, a being that is not constituted in and through consciousness but that instead somehow constitutes consciousness. (Wojtyla, 1993, pp. 225-226)

Thus, for Wojtyla, the existence of the person is presupposed. From this point of departure, he is able to move into his investigation of the ontological structure of the person and from there onto the discussion of how the person relates with and towards other persons and reality in general. It should be noted, however, that while Wojtyla does reject the absolutization of consciousness, he clearly sees consciousness as an intrinsic and constitutive element of the person (Buttiglione, 1997, pp. 129-130).

In speaking of the human person, Wojtyla maintains that there is an ontic unity in the person. This unity allows the person to be an "I" and not merely a collection of parts. This unity includes all physical and spiritual aspects of the person and therefore, to Wojtyla, it is never possible to discount any aspect of the person as being unimportant. He writes that in an analysis of the person there is "the need for a deeper insight into the psychosomatic complexity of man and into the complexity of the dynamisms of both his somatic and psychical aspects" (Wojtyla, 1979a, p. 199). It is in the noting of this ontic unity and complexity that Emmanuel Mounier's influence on Wojtyla is quite evident (Mounier, 1970, pp. 3-16).

The realization of this unity and the resultant realization of the complexity of the person leads Wojtyla to issue a caveat: the human person must never be treated as a mere object of experience or object to be studied. This treatment would be beneath the dignity of the person since it implies that the person is just one more unknown to be unraveled by the human intellect. The person is, qua person, always to be related to as a subject, as another person. He notes that while "having conquered so many secrets of nature the conqueror himself must have his own mysteries unraveled anew" and that there is the danger of him "becoming usual and commonplace; he risks becoming too ordinary even for himself" (Wojtyla, 1979a, p. 22). Having given this warning, Wojtyla adds that his study of the person "was borne out of that wonderment at the human being which... initiates the first cognitive impulse" and that "[m]an should not lose his proper place in the world that he has shaped himself" (Wojtyla, 1979a, p. 22). This understanding of the person as subject and not object has Kantian overtones, but is very much in keeping with personalism. Wojtyla returns frequently to this theme in his later works, both before and after becoming pope.

The Person and Act. Wojtyla has set out, through his philosophical investigations, to attempt to unravel the mystery that is the human person. He argues that the moment when persons are most visibly being persons is when they are performing human acts. A human act is an action that is carried out in freedom and based upon a particular value assigned to the action by the person performing it. When performing a human act, the person is "self-possessed." It can be said that a person performing a human act is conscious of the action on three levels: as the performer of the action, as the cause of the action and as an objective observer of the action being performed. Wojtyla has described these three levels as the *reflexive function* of the person: defined more simply, the person is conscious of self, conscious of self and an other, and conscious of being conscious of self and an other. These three levels of consciousness do not imply a lack of unity within the person; it is still a particular "I" that is acting, but the levels do imply that performing a human act involves every aspect of the person: mind, body, soul, emotions, etc.

Since the act involves the entire person, Wojtyla argues, and is done in freedom and with deliberation, a human act can always be said to be either good or bad; either in accord with, or contrary to, personalistic values. It is possible to argue that not all persons have the same set of values and therefore that this particular claim is invalid. This argument misses Wojtyla's point completely. Human experience shows that human acts are performed based upon *some* value system; a person chooses one way of acting because it is of higher value to that person than another way of acting. While Wojtyla would clearly maintain the existence of an objective truth, Natural Law, and Divine Law, his philosophical position does not rest upon them, but rather upon the findings of his phenomenological methodology.

Since a human act can be said to be either good or bad, Wojtyla argues that persons themselves not only perform good or bad acts, but actually experience themselves as good or bad. This idea is grounded in the reflexive function of the person. Wojtyla (1979a) writes,

> It is also in connection with his acting (that is, action) that man experiences as his own the moral value of good or bad. He experiences them in the attitude he assumes toward them, an attitude that is at once emotional and appreciative. At any rate, he is not only conscious of the morality of his actions but he actually experiences it, often very deeply. (p. 48)

The point here is that *freely* chosen human acts contribute to the development process of the human person. A person's actions contribute to the actualization of his or her potentiality, or to use Wojtyla's phrase, self-fulfillment. Persons performing human acts show, both to themselves and to other persons, the very reality of who they are. Wojtyla adds that any act of freedom brings with it certain responsibilities which the person must acknowledge when choosing to act in a certain way.

The Person and Transcendence. Having presented the manner in which persons can more fully actualize their potentiality, Wojtyla is able to put forward the idea that it is a person's ability to *transcend* oneself in one's act that realizes one's personhood. Transcendence is being able to freely choose to move out of oneself, whether toward the world around us (horizontal transcendence) or toward higher values (vertical transcendence). Whether horizontal or vertical, the goal of transcendence is the same: experiencing the ability to freely act to move toward a greater self-fulfillment. Seeking to interpret Wojtyla's meaning of transcendence, Kenneth Schmitz (1993) explains,

> Part of our fulfillment consists in a horizontal transcendence, that is, in our going
> out to the things around us, in coming to know them, in interacting with them
> and being affected by them. But such horizontal transcendence is only a con-
> dition of our fulfillment...The threshold we must cross is upwards; it lies beyond
> us. We are called to vertical transcendence, in the sense that we are called to
> progress toward the highest realization of values. In this way, genuine change
> takes place in us, as we return to ourselves, once we have surrendered the self
> that we presently are to the self that we might become. (p. 86)

Persons, because they have free choice, are able to choose to remain
isolated within themselves and to reject transcendence. This rejection
leads to isolation and loneliness, the opposites of the highest values of
persons: community and love.

Being able to act in freedom is the only state of affairs which is worthy
of the human person. Not having this freedom prevents a person from
being able to fully express one's personhood and fully "be" a person.
Wojtyla will also clearly point out that this freedom is not a freedom to do
whatever one wants whenever one wants. This freedom is the ability to
vertically transcend the person one currently is and move toward higher
values, the highest value being love. Because it is possible that the person
may be in error and make wrong choices, freedom, states Wojtyla, must
always be at the service of the truth (Whenever and wherever
encountered, the word "truth," as used by Wojtyla, should be understood
to mean "objective truth" as used philosophically, unless otherwise
indicated). When freedom and truth are united, a person's choices and
acts will lead towards ever higher goods and transcendence and thus
toward ever greater fulfillment as a person. The danger is clearly that truth
and freedom can be, and often are, separated, in which case the acts of a
person are directed toward the bad, thereby leading to a diminishment of
the person.

It is in asking the question as to the ultimate end of this transcendence
that Wojtyla the philosopher becomes Wojtyla the theologian and pastor.
Moving from the purely philosophical, Wojtyla begins to present the
ultimate tie which human persons have to God. It would appear that
Wojtyla may envision the ideal person, existing as if in some Platonic
"world of forms," that all persons are striving to become. This, however, is
not the case. Wojtyla believes that human qualities, whether physical,
intellectual, spiritual, emotional, etc., cannot exist outside of a human
person. Therefore, there is no Platonic form of the perfect person. For
Wojtyla, the ultimate end of vertical transcendence is the highest good,

God himself, or Love. Thus, all human persons are continually called out of themselves toward the love of God in the community of the Trinity.

Additionally, although he does not envision an "ideal person" in the manner of Platonic thought, Wojtyla does present the God-man, Jesus Christ, as the model for all human persons to emulate. In coming to know Jesus, the human person is able to know what it means to be a fully actualized person. Wojtyla brought this understanding of Jesus to the fore in his first encyclical as pope. He wrote that if a person wishes to thoroughly understand self, then,

> he must with his unrest, uncertainty and even his weakness and sinfulness, with his life and death, draw near to Christ. He must, so to speak, enter into Him with all his own self, he must "appropriate" and assimilate the whole of the reality of the Incarnation and Redemption in order to find himself. (Wojtyla/John Paul II, 1979c, No. 10)

Jesus is, therefore, looked to be the center of all human history because it is he who can be the model for persons to follow in their efforts at transcending self. It is important to realize as well that Wojtyla does not limit the ability to transcend self to believers in Jesus Christ. The ability to transcend self is an ability of the human person and therefore is possible without Jesus or the grace of God. More will be said regarding Jesus as the model in the discussion of the role of the student in the educative process in Chapter V.

The Person and Integration. As has been seen above, the ability of the person to transcend self by the free acts one chooses is what reveals the person and enables the person to actualize one's potential as a human person. Having established this, Wojtyla explains what is necessary, on the part of the individual person, to allow the process of transcendence to take place. What is necessary is integration.

Integration occurs when all aspects of the person, whether psychic or somatic, are united or blended together on the level of the person. This unity is much more significant than speaking of soul and body joined; the unity is now such that the experience of the person is that "I act." Wojtyla explains that integration occurs when,

> The psyche and the soma take an active part...not at their own levels but *at the level of the person*. Thus also in this case integration means introduction to a higher level of unity than that indicated in the expression 'psychosomatic unity' taken in its empirical sense...This does not mean, however, that they cease to be in some way distinct. On the contrary, they continue to exist in their own right and essentially co-create the dynamic reality of the person's action. (Wojtyla, 1979a, p. 198)

Integration is what enables the person to make the free choices towards higher values necessary to transcend oneself. As the ability of persons to be fully integrated decreases, so does the ability of persons to fully actualize their potential *as* persons.

Thus, there are many obstacles, whether psychic, somatic or spiritual which would tend to inhibit the person's ability to be integrated. While this inability does not reduce the dignity due to the person *qua* person, it does hinder the ability to move towards being fully actualized as a person. All variety of mental and physical illness could be a hindrance unless the person is able to move past these obstacles toward wholeness. In commenting on Wojtyla, Seifert (1981) offers this example:

> A person who fails to relate properly to his body, who fails to bodily express his intentions, his concerns, his love fails to be fully integrated. Many persons suffer from inhibitions, neuroses, or wrong attitudes in virtue of which they are unable to express their inner life. (p. 29)

The person must, through continued effort throughout life, work at allowing all aspects of self to enter into the process of acting. An act which fails to take into account the fullness of the person does not lead to transcendence and integration. Integration, and also transcendence, is not a one time event, but a continuing process throughout the life of the person. This understanding of integration, on Wojtyla's part, underscores his personalist approach to the unity of body and soul. The human person is once again held to be more than the sum of aggregate parts.

The Person and Knowing. Although Wojtyla does not present a fully developed epistemology, it is safe to say that his approach to how a person knows follows traditional Thomistic lines. What is important to note here, however, is that Wojtyla is careful to argue against the prevailing trend in modern philosophy that persons are only able to know their own minds.

Wojtyla holds that although unique, each person is able to have a genuine exchange of knowledge with other persons. This occurs through the action of the other.

When persons perform human acts, Wojtyla points out, they are opening themselves up to being known by others because the act performed reveals some aspect of the very personhood of the actor. Persons are able to come to know other persons because of their experience of themselves as self-reflective, conscious human persons. Thus every human act performed by another person allows one to come to an ever richer knowledge of that person. It can be said, therefore, that learning is a deeply personal exchange: persons do not just share information with each other, they share knowledge of their very selves. Although one person will never be able to fully know the other, it is possible to speak of sharing knowledge which is on a higher level then sense data and empirical investigation. Also, Wojtyla implies that, when speaking of knowing any objective truth, it must be remembered that objective truth is only apprehended by subjective persons. This approach to human knowledge will have an important impact upon the process of education, as will be seen.

The Relationship Between Faith and Reason. When speaking of knowledge and the human person from a Catholic Christian philosopher such as Wojtyla, one must also take into account the relationship between human knowledge (reason) and response to divine revelation (faith). This relationship will also influence the educative process, and therefore it is important to note Wojtyla's understanding of their relationship. It is indeed fortunate that one of his latest encyclicals, *Fides et Ratio* (Wojtyla/ John Paul II, 1998a), deals with precisely this issue.

For Wojtyla, taking the position of Saint Thomas, there is no opposition between faith and reason because there is only one truth. Whether a person arrives at this truth by human reason or by placing faith in divine revelation is of little importance; what does have importance is that it is the truth. Obviously, as soon as one discusses issues of truth, there arises the question as to whether there is an universally valid truth, and if there is, is this truth knowable by the human person? For Wojtyla, the answer is that there is a universal truth and that it is knowable. Wojtyla's position on this issue is clear even from his presentation on the transcendence of the person. In order to transcend the self, the person must be looking towards the higher value and freely choose. The notion of value and free choice presuppose, for Wojtyla, the existence of a universally valid truth. Ultimately, then, faith and reason are, for Wojtyla, simply two roads leading to the same destination. What is important is not to set them up as contradicting entities, for this leads to errors of great consequence, but rather to set them as complementary entities which will allow each person to come to knowledge of the truth (Wojtyla/John Paul II, 1998a).

Another issue regarding faith and reason which comes into view, especially when speaking of the education of young people, is the position that faith and reason are to be kept separate under the guise that religion has no place in science or science no place in religion. Neither pure reason (rationalism) nor pure faith (fideism), taken alone, is worthy of the human person, since singly they do not relate to the full reality (ontic unity of body and soul) of the person. By preventing the integration of these two roads to truth, the human person is done a disservice. It is in taking this stance that Wojtyla demonstrates that his thought takes an opposing position to that of Modern philosophy, which does not allot to faith any place in rational thought. More will be said of this opposition between Wojtyla and Modern philosophical thought below.

Critiques of Wojtyla's Philosophy of the Person

Wojtyla and Modern Philosophy. From the outset, it is clear that Wojtyla begins his philosophical discussion concerning the human person from a metaphysical perspective, a perspective firmly rooted in Thomas Aquinas' metaphysics. Even though Wojtyla approaches his metaphysical discussion using a phenomenological methodology, the very fact that he maintains the validity of metaphysics as a framework for discussing the mode of being of the human person, places him at odds with Modern philosophy.

Coming into existence during the Age of Reason, Modern philosophy began to question the validity of any knowledge which was not arrived at through the use of the scientific method. Thus, if something could not be "proven" by experimentation, the something could not be considered to be validly knowable. Flowing from this notion was the understanding that human persons could only be said to know their own minds regarding any idea which was not part of the body of scientific knowledge. It is clear that, by accepting these two concepts of knowledge, Modern philosophy effecttively dismantled the science of metaphysics. Thus, the validity of Wojtyla's seeking to approach a discussion of the human person by relying upon Thomistic metaphysics can be called into question.

Wojtyla himself has acknowledged that his philosophical approach is contrary to many of the ideas of Modern philosophy. Obviously he offers a critique of the methods and conclusions brought to philosophical thought by the Modern philosophers. In *Crossing the Threshold of Hope*, Wojtyla presents his belief that the move away from metaphysics as a valid path to true knowledge began with Descartes. He writes that Descartes, "distances us from the philosophy of existence, and also from the traditional approaches of Saint Thomas which lead to God who is 'autonomous existence'" (Wojtyla/John Paul II, 1994c, p. 51). It is this distancing which Wojtyla sees as moving philosophical thought away from concentrating upon objective existence toward concentrating on subjective knowledge and consciousness. He argues against the dismantling of metaphysics by noting that a being cannot have consciousness unless it has existence; therefore the Cartesian axiom of "I think, therefore I am" would, according to Wojtyla's line of thought, be better stated as "I am, therefore I think."

Although Wojtyla sees Descartes as being the progenitor of this move away from metaphysics towards a concentration on knowledge, he also notes that, "Kant is the most notable representative of this movement" (Wojtyla/John Paul II, 1994c, p. 52). It should be recalled that one of the aspects of Max Scheler's work which Wojtyla found attractive was Scheler's critique of the Kantian approach to knowledge. While the phenomenologists would have their own difficulties with Wojtyla's metaphysics, it is interesting to note that they would share with Wojtyla a concern about the conclusions which modern philosophy came to. A concern which was shared with postmodern thinkers as well.

Wojtyla and Postmodernism. Although there are a number of areas in which Wojtyla's philosophical anthropology is open to criticism, the most potentially damaging comes from postmodern thought. In a few pages it is nearly impossible to give even a sketchy outline of current postmodernism; what will be attempted, however, is to note where the main criticisms of Wojtyla's work stem from and to give a brief explanation of the ideas which make up these criticisms.

When speaking of postmodernism, the first difficulty which one encounters is identifying and presenting a reasonably succinct definition of what postmodernism is. Charles Jencks notes this confusion when he writes that in postmodernism there is a,

> tendency among philosophers to discuss all Post-Positivist thinkers together as Post-Modern whether or not they have anything more in common than a rejection of Modern Logical Positivism. Thus there are two quite different meanings to the term and a general confusion which is not confined to the public. (Jencks, 1986, pp. 8–9)

What seems to be common to postmodern thinkers is that the world-view of the Modern era is no longer valid in its overall attempt to provide "metanarratives" which seek to neatly package all human life, experience, and knowledge. The invalidity of Modern thought can be seen in its results: the depersonalization of humanity, ethnic hatred, the horrors of two World Wars and the Holocaust, global warming and ecological neglect, just to name a few. In the process of performing this packaging, artificial divisions were created between branches of science which brought about disunity, not only concerning human thought, but also human beings. Postmodernism also seeks to celebrate and acknowledge the diversity of peoples (gender, race, nationality, etc.) which will lead to full acceptance of all people. Additionally, the postmodern effort is also aimed at establishing the rightful place of humankind as part of the earth's ecosystem, not the master of it.

As was mentioned by Jencks (1986), there are two distinct paths which postmodern thought has taken. The first, towards deconstruction, can be considered the more radical of the two. It seeks to "deconstruct" the great metanarratives (or "world stories") of the Modern era which, at best, burdened humankind or, at worst, enslaved all or most of humankind. An example of one of these metanarratives is western philosophy (specifically metaphysics) which sought (seeks) to reconcile apparent diversity into some form of unity. Tracing the development of deconstructionist thought from Descartes through Husserl to Nietzsche, Mark Taylor is able to say that, there are no facts, "only interpretations." The notion of an independent truth or true world beyond the realm of appearances is a construction or projection that grows out of the effort to escape the flux of becoming and repress the disruptive movement of time...[T]he search for truth is actually an exercise of "the will to power" through which one tries to master the uncertainties of the human condition by repressing the inevitability of fragmentation and dislocation. (Taylor, 1986, p. 16)

It is from this heritage that deconstructionists like Jacques Derrida seek to do away with the metanarratives of western thought, including philosophy and the Judeo-Christian Scriptures (i.e., "salvation history").

Metaphysics, as a specific branch of philosophy, because it seeks to investigate precisely what was done away with from the Modern era (the search for truth and reconciling unity and diversity), is also put aside and said to have come to an end. Taylor notes, "The search for grounding presence comes to its conclusion in modern philosophy. More specifically, metaphysics ends with the philosophy of the subject identified by Descartes and completed by Hegel and Husserl" (Taylor, 1986, p. 18). Jean-Francois Lyotard concurs with the need to do away with metaphysics, but also warns against going too far in the direction of positivism. He writes, "We must follow metaphysics in its fall...but without lapsing into the current mood of positivist pragmatism, which, beneath its liberal exterior, is no less hegemonic than dogmatism" (Lyotard, 1993, pp. 65–66). Thus, while deconstructionists tend to sound very negative, they seek the same goals mentioned above regarding postmodernism and are not unanimous in their approach to deconstruction.

The other "branch" of postmodernism can be classified as constructionist. This group of thinkers put forward the same criticisms of the Modern era as do the deconstructionists, along with the goals of postmodernism spoken of above. The constructionists believe that the,

postmodernism of political and feminist writers who have been inspired by Martin Heidegger, Jacques Derrida, and Michel Foucault is really an anti-worldview because it deconstructs and eliminates the elements necessary for a world view, such as God, self, purpose, meaning, and truth as correspondence [between subjective idea and reality]...the potential result of deconstruction [is] relativism and nihilism. (Slattery, 1995, p. 30)

In their desire to retain the good elements of the pre-modern and modern eras, the constructionists are viewed by their deconstructionist colleagues as being no better than the "moderns" they seek to critique. Despite the rather harsh criticisms leveled against them, the constructionists continue their efforts to have a postmodernism which, "regards the world as an organism rather than as a machine, the earth as a home rather than as a functional possession, and persons as interdependent rather than as isolated and independent" (Slattery, 1995, p. 19).

While the above presentation of postmodernism barely scratches the surface of the intricacies of this school of thought, it has presented the issues upon which to base postmodernism's critique of Wojtyla's philosophical anthropology. Deconstructive postmodernism presents the greatest challenge to the validity of Wojtyla's metaphysical presentation, precisely because it calls into question the validity of metaphysics as a science and objective truth as a reality. Both the possibility of "doing" metaphysics and the existence of objective truth is central to Wojtyla's philosophy in general and to his thinking regarding education, in particular. Schmitz notes the questions which deconstructionism presents to philosophers of today. He writes,

> Deconstruction is part of a wider critical re-examination of nothing less than the nature and limits of rationality...In its skepticism and, in more extreme instances, its nihilism, deconstruction strikes at the very core of long-held understandings of the philosophical enterprise...The very possibility of continuing the long conversation we call Western culture and Western civilization is, therefore, itself called into question. (Schmitz, 1989, pp. 69–70)

How, then, does Wojtyla respond to the postmodern critique of his philosophical ideas?

In the first place, it should be noted that Wojtyla would fully agree with the overall assessment put forward by postmodern thinkers regarding the inadequacies and harm which much of the modern era has visited upon humanity, particularly regarding the dehumanization of the person, ethnic and racial hatred and warfare, and the misuse of earth's ecosystem (Wojtyla/John Paul II, 1985, No. 15). He would, however, fully disagree with the dismissal of the value of metaphysics and the existence of a knowable objective truth.

Wojtyla argues that, based upon universal human experience of the desire to seek and know the truth, that this truth exists and that philosophy itself was born from this very experience. He writes,

> Although times change and knowledge increases, it is possible to discern a core philosophical insight within the history of thought as a whole. Consider, for example, the principles of non-contradiction, finality and causality, as well as the concept of the person as a free and intelligent subject...These are among the indications that, beyond different schools of thought, there exists a body of knowledge which may be judged a kind of spiritual heritage of humanity. (Wojtyla/John Paul II, 1998a, Nos. 3-4)

Thus, using the methodology of phenomenology, which has been his tool from the beginning of his philosophical explorations, Wojtyla believes that he is on very solid ground when he asserts the validity and existence of a universal truth knowable to human persons. In addition, he adds that because of a one-sided emphasis on the subjectivity of human reason, "[a] legitimate plurality of positions has yielded to an undifferentiated pluralism, based upon the assumption that all positions are equally valid... On this understanding, everything is reduced to opinion" (Wojtyla/John Paul II, 1998a, No. 5).

Wojtyla's response to the validity of metaphysical thought also rests upon the ideas quoted in the preceding paragraph. Since human nature, in itself, seeks to come to a knowledge of being itself, the science whereby being is investigated must retain its validity. By moving away from metaphysics, current philosophical thought has done a disservice to humanity. He writes,

> Abandoning the investigation of being, modern philosophical research has concentrated instead upon human knowing. Rather than make use of the human capacity to know the truth, modern philosophy has preferred to accentuate the ways in which this capacity is limited and conditioned. (Wojtyla/John Paul II, 1998a, No. 5)

Just as human experience is used to validate the existence of an objective truth, Wojtyla makes use of experience to validate the worth of metaphysical inquiry.

Wojtyla and Phenomenology. Because Wojtyla has chosen to make use of phenomenological methodology to examine the ontic reality which is the human person, his philosophy has been referred to as phenomenological personalism. An issue which has been raised, from phenomenologists, is whether Wojtyla's philosophy can be described as phenomenology at all since he appears to be, when all is said and done, a Thomistic personalist cloaking his philosophy in phenomenological terminology.

Edmund Husserl, the founder of the phenomenology, had a number of rather prominent, first generation, disciples. Among these disciples were Edith Stein, Max Scheler, and Roman Ingarden. Stein and Scheler have both been discussed above, as to their influence upon Wojtyla. Roman Ingarden, however, also played an influential role in the formation of Wojtyla's thought and it is this role which will help make clear that Wojtyla's use of the phenomenological method is very much a valid approach. Ingarden, a Pole who spent his teaching career at the University of Lublin, can best be described as a disciple of Husserl's early thought (Buttiglione, 1997, p. 54). Husserl's move toward Idealism caused the break between himself and Ingarden as Ingarden did not wish to move away from Realism. It was at this point that Ingarden began to appreciate the methodology of phenomenology as a tool to help further the understanding of the human person. Buttiglione (1997) has noted that,

> For Ingarden, phenomenology is not a philosophical system but a method of philosophical inquiry which can be applied in diverse ways and which can work together with the most diverse philosophies. Ingarden himself maintained a fundamentally realistic direction. (p. 55)

Wojtyla's view of phenomenology as a method can be seen, therefore, to have come from his countryman who was a student of Husserl himself.

With this understanding, the criticism that Wojtyla is not faithful to what phenomenology is about is not wholly valid when one realizes that Wojtyla has chosen to associate himself with the phenomenological realism of Roman Ingarden and to make use of phenomenology as a method as Ingarden did. This branch of phenomenology distanced itself from Husserl's original work, as was indicated above, and does not claim that an individual's experience is normative. Thus, Wojtyla's use of experience to gain insight into the person is valid, as a method, within this particular branch of phenomenology and can work well with Wojtyla's Thomistic metaphysics. Additionally, Wojtyla's view that in examining the act of a person one can gain true knowledge of that person clearly sets him within the limits of phenomenological thought today.

It should also be noted that Wojtyla's major contribution to philosophy, especially in Poland, has been to bring about a re-examination of traditional Thomistic metaphysics in light of the phenomenological insights of Roman Ingarden. George McLean (1994) states, concerning philosophy in Poland, that,

> One of its branches, by its solid grounding in tradition, reflects the perennial search for the most profound and important truths...[A]nother of its branches situates itself in, develops and draws its dynamism from the contemporary vision of the person. Philosophers in Poland, inspired by the work of Roman Ingarden and led by Cardinal Karol Wojtyla, richly explored this inspiration. (p. vii)

Given Wojtyla's contribution in seeking to re-present traditional metaphysics and the extensive nature with which the phenomenological method has been used in Polish philosophical circles, his approach would appear to be valid.

Although these critiques are not exhaustive of the possible areas of criticism of Wojtyla's philosophy, they reflect those specific difficulties which one may encounter. They are presented here so that they can be kept in mind as Wojtyla's philosophy of education is examined in the succeeding pages.

IV

THE PERSON AND EDUCATION

The previous chapter introduced the reader to Wojtyla's philosophical anthropology. There it was possible to discern the view that a human being is, by nature, a person. As a person, the human being possesses a dignity which must be respected and is also called to be a participating member of a community. This participation in community with other persons is predicated upon the person's ability to transcend self based upon a movement toward higher values. Persons can be said to fulfill themselves as persons when they act in harmony with the values which lead to an ever greater transcendence. These acts reveal the person *qua* person and allow for persons to know each other and share knowledge.

With Wojtyla's understanding of the person thus presented, it is now possible to move into the main area under investigation: what does Wojtyla envision as the role played by education in the life of the human person and how can this educative process best be carried out? As has been noted previously, Wojtyla has never written a philosophy of education, and therefore it is necessary to compile his understanding of the educative process from his various writings and allocutions. This is possible thanks to the consistency Wojtyla maintains in his use of terminology; when a term is used, it is used to convey the same meaning in all variety of texts.

The following excerpt, from one of Wojtyla's papal allocutions, provides a fine introduction to his overall understanding of education which will be examined in this chapter and is therefore worth quoting at length:

> In education, to which, together with the parents, the school and other organisms of society contribute, the child must find the possibilities "of developing in a healthy, normal way on the physical, intellectual, moral, spiritual, and social plane, in conditions of freedom and dignity."
>
> The child also has the right to the truth, in teaching that takes into account the fundamental ethical values, and that will make possible a spiritual education, in conformity with the religion to which the child belongs, the orientation legitimately desired by his parents and the exigencies of freedom of conscience.
>
> To speak of the rights of the child is to speak of the duties of parents and educators, who remain in the service of the child, of his higher interests. But the

growing child must take part himself in his own development, with responsibilities that correspond to his capacities; and care must be taken not to neglect to speak to him also of his own duties toward others and toward society. (Wojtyla/John Paul II, 1979d, pp. 128-129)

As can be seen, this quote provides a clear presentation of Wojtyla's overall understanding of education. What follows is an exposition of the pertinent elements of the ideas presented.

Purpose of Education

Before it is possible to even discuss what elements are involved in the educative process, the ultimate philosophical end of this process must be established. It is in establishing this ultimate end, or purpose, of education that Wojtyla's personalism is most evident. Sounding very much like Jacques Maritain (1943), Wojtyla proposes that the purpose of education is to assist the young person in becoming a fulfilled human person: by which Wojtyla means a person capable of acting freely to choose the good, of horizontal and vertical transcendence, and participation in whatever communities of persons of which he is a member (Wojtyla/John Paul II, 1979d, pp. 128-129).

This being said, Wojtyla's understanding of education has progressed from Maritain's emphasis upon education being concerned mainly with the development of the intellect of the person (Maritain, 1943). While Maritain does speak of education being concerned with the whole person, he does not develop this concept to the same extent as Wojtyla does. Very much in keeping with his own philosophical approach to the person, Wojtyla never refers to education as being a process directed at the intellect, but rather toward the entire human person. In speaking with Catholic school teachers in New Orleans in 1987, Wojtyla stated that

by accepting and developing the legacy of Catholic thought and educational experience which they [lay Catholic teachers] have inherited, they take their place as full partners in the Church's mission of educating the whole person and of transmitting the good news of salvation in Jesus Christ to successive generations of young Americans. (Wojtyla/John Paul II, 1987b, p. 154)

For Wojtyla, as has been detailed in Chapter III, the "whole person" refers to the complex mystery which is each individual person. Education can never be viewed as only a process of forming the intellect because the intellect is only one aspect of the human person.

When speaking of Catholic education, Wojtyla does maintain that the "ultimate goal of all Catholic education is salvation in Jesus Christ" (Wojtyla/John Paul II, 1987b, p. 155). This expressed goal would seem to imply that the purpose of Catholic education is to produce a new generation of Catholics who would continue to maintain the existence of the Church. Wojtyla, however, would not agree with this interpretation of his use of the term "goal," since it would be antithetical to his understanding of the person. As was presented in Chapter III, the human person may never be looked upon as an object to be used by another person. If the purpose of Catholic education was simply to produce new generations of Church members, the young persons would be in the position of being used by the school for its own purposes. They would effectively become objects of use by, and not subjects in relation to, other persons. This view would be unacceptable to Wojtyla since he sees the purpose of education to be assisting the person to come to self-fulfillment. He writes that,

> This is also the purpose of education, both the education of children, and the mutual education of adults; it is just that—a matter of seeking true ends, i.e. real goods as the ends of our actions, and of finding and showing to others the ways to realize them. But in this educational activity, especially when we have to do with the upbringing of young children, we must never treat a person as a means to an end. This principle has universal validity. (Wojtyla, 1981b, p. 27)

How, then, does the "goal" mentioned by Wojtyla fit into the purpose of education Wojtyla puts forward?

Wojtyla would answer by pointing out that the Catholic school presents Jesus Christ to the student as the person who would help them fulfill themselves as persons. In his Letter to Families, Wojtyla writes that,

> through Christ all education, within the family and outside of it, becomes part of God's own saving pedagogy, which is addressed to individuals and families and culminates in the paschal mystery of the Lord's death and resurrection. The heart of our redemption is the starting point of every process of Christian education, which likewise is always an education to a full humanity. (Wojtyla /John Paul II, 1994b, No. 16)

This presentation of the person of Jesus is done to further the overall end or purpose of education: helping the young person fulfill his personhood. Wojtyla explains to teachers that,

> By enriching your students' lives with the fullness of Christ's message and by inviting them to accept with all their hearts Christ's work, which is the Church, you promote most effectively their integral human development and you help them to build a community of faith, hope and love. (Wojtyla/John Paul II, 1987b, p. 155)

It is important to note that Wojtyla uses the term "inviting" when speaking of the acceptance of Christ and his work. Students must always be given the freedom to choose to believe on their own; to be forced into the act of belief would not be worthy of the human person, and it would not be a human act. Wojtyla is very clear on this point when he writes, in *Catechesi Tradendae*, that,

> from the view point of human rights, every human being has the right to seek religious truth and adhere to it freely, that is to say, "without coercion on the part of individuals or of social groups and any human power," in such a way that in this matter of religion, 'no one is to be forced to act against his or her conscience or prevented from acting in conformity to it. (Wojtyla/John Paul II, 1979b, No. 14)

Thus, while Catholic schools may well set as a goal the personal acceptance of Jesus by each student, this acceptance does not indicate that the purpose of Catholic education has been achieved. The purpose of Catholic education has been achieved if, and only if, this acceptance of Jesus is done as a freely chosen act directed toward vertical transcendence, personal integration, and self-fulfillment.

When studying the various writings of Wojtyla concerning education, it becomes obvious that he believes there is a responsibility upon the educated person to actively work toward the betterment of human society and culture. This call to the educated person to accept a social responsibility could be construed to mean that education has a social goal, that is, the betterment of society. Here, as above when speaking about Catholic education passing on the faith, Wojtyla understands that educated persons will, as a consequence of their education, bring about a better society. The betterment of society is not a goal, or end, of education, but rather a natural consequence of education.

Self-Education

As has been shown, the role of the individual person in shaping his own life by free human acts and transcendence is a central point of Wojtyla's philosophical anthropology. This being the case, the active role in the educative process is clearly with the student; it is not so much that the student is taught, but that the student learns. It is only this active role in the learning process which is worthy of the human person. A mere passive indoctrination would remove the element of freedom from the student and inhibit his ability to become self-fulfilled. This should not be taken to imply that the role of the educators is a passive one, because it is not. It would be better to speak of the process of education itself as being an active one, on the part of both students and educators. Wojtyla does, however, speak much more about the need for students to take an active role in the process of their own education.

Wojtyla refers to this active role in the educative process as *self-education*. Although parents and teachers may present to the child various ideas through their words and actions, it is the child who must make this example his own. In his *Letter to Families*, Wojtyla writes,

> The process of education ultimately leads to the phase of self-education, which occurs when the individual, after attaining an appropriate level of psychophysical maturity, begins to "educate himself on his own."...Even so, the process of self-education cannot fail to be marked by the educational influence which the family and school have on children and adolescents. (Wojtyla/John Paul II, 1994a, No. 16)

This understanding of education being active on the part of students flows naturally from Wojtyla's philosophy. Also, it is important to see this self-education as a process which the child gradually takes upon himself, and not as something innately present in the new-born human person.

The process of self-education begins in the home, continues in the school, and remains a life-long task. Wojtyla clearly understands self-education as being an ongoing process, one not just limited to the young person, and which also has elements of reciprocity involved in it. He writes,

> As the children mature, the task of education turns into self-education. The parents, in turn, who are their children's natural educators, also themselves continue to be educated by their children as they carry out their parental

functions at the different stages of their children's development. (Wojtyla, 1993, p. 336)

Here again, Wojtyla's vision of the purpose of education being the movement towards self-fulfillment of the person is exemplified. Because the processes of transcendence, integration, and self-fulfillment must continue throughout a person's life, it is only natural that the educational process must be life-long as well. More will be said regarding self-education in Chapter VI, as the role of the student is explored through Wojtyla's writings to young people.

This life-long educational process presupposes, for Wojtyla, that the person, whether young or older, is part of a community. While the entire issue of family and community in the educational process will be examined at length in the succeeding chapter, it is introduced here because of the integral part which community plays in education. It is not possible to speak of educating the person without reference to the communities in which the person is a participating member.

Seeking Truth Through Education

As has been shown in Chapter III, Wojtyla's philosophy of the person is predicated upon Thomistic metaphysics. It is here that Wojtyla's belief in an objectively knowable truth is grounded. His understanding of the relationship between truth and self-fulfillment must also be kept in mind. A person who consistently makes choices which are at odds with the truth is not directed at self-fulfillment or integration. Thus, the process of education must be one in which the student is consistently called upon to relate one's life and actions to the objective order of reality (truth). What must come into play, therefore, is an appreciation for the objective moral order and the need to transcend oneself so as to bring oneself ever closer to the truth.

This being the case, education and educators must always seek to present to the students the desirability of seeking the truth so that they are able to move toward self-fulfillment. Wojtyla writes, "Even if they [teachers] do not 'teach religion,' their service in a Catholic school is part of the Church's unceasing endeavor to lead all to 'profess the truth in love and grow to the full maturity of Christ the head' (Eph. 4:15)" (Wojtyla/John Paul II, 1987b, p. 154). When students come to profess the truth, they are well on the road toward personal integration and fulfillment.

In addition to assisting the student in coming to an understanding of the need to relate one's life to the truth, the educative process must also seek to present to the student the unified nature of truth. This is done by an integration of all the various curricula and by avoiding setting up artificial divisions between the various academic disciplines. In his Apostolic Constitution, *Ex Corde Ecclesiae*, Wojtyla writes that, although the integration of knowledge is a process which will always remain incomplete,

> the exposition of knowledge in recent decades, together with the rigid compartmentalization of knowledge within individual academic disciplines, makes the task increasingly difficult...It is necessary to work toward a higher synthesis of knowledge, in which alone lies the possibility of satisfying that thirst for truth which is profoundly inscribed on the heart of the human person. (Wojtyla/John Paul II, 1990a, No. 16)

The truth, then, is not something that any one discipline can claim as its own or can claim to fully present in its entirety. It is an entity unto itself which each discipline can help to explicate. Clearly, then, for Wojtyla, the educational enterprise must assist the student in understanding this basic understanding of the unity of truth.

There is the danger, when speaking of the objective nature of the truth, to imagine that Wojtyla sees the truth as a disembodied reality existing unto itself. For Wojtyla, truth finds its full existence in God. Ultimately, then, the search for truth is the search for God; a person is able to find the fullness of truth when he enters into a relationship with God (Wojtyla/John Paul II, 1994a). It is for this reason that Wojtyla will, as was presented earlier, assert the fundamental unity of faith and reason. He writes, "Religious faith calls for intellectual inquiry; and the confidence that there can be no contradiction between faith and reason is a distinctive feature of the Catholic humanistic tradition as it existed in the past and as it exists in our own day" (Wojtyla/John Paul II, 1987c, p. 162).

An ancillary point, though important when discussing education, which Wojtyla makes with regard to truth is the role of pluralism. The issue is how does the educator deal with bringing the student to a knowledge of the truth when so many diverse opinions exist on what constitutes truth, if it indeed exists at all. Wojtyla's understanding of this situation is that this diversity does not deny the existence of truth, but is a means to continuing to seek the truth. He writes,

> Modern culture is marked by a pluralism of attitudes, points of view and insights. This situation rightly requires mutual understanding; it means that society and groups within society must respect those who have different outlooks from their own. But pluralism does not exist for its own sake; it is directed to the fullness of truth. (Wojtyla/John Paul II, 1987c, p. 162)

From this statement it becomes clear that truth is well served when there is dialogue concerning the various opinions expresses. Wojtyla sees this dialogical process as eventually leading all concerned to the truth. This being said, Wojtyla also cautions about the tendency to accept as valid all opinions without attempting to come to a resolution as to where the truth lies. He notes that,

> In the academic context, the respect for persons which pluralism rightly envisions does not justify the view that ultimate questions about human life and destiny have no final answers or that all beliefs are of equal value, provided that none is asserted as absolutely true and normative. Truth is not served in this way. (Wojtyla/John Paul II, 1987c, p. 162)

It is clear that, for Wojtyla, the educational process is one of continually seeking for the truth, not an acceptance of all opinions as true nor the assumption that the truth cannot be known by the human mind (Wojtyla/John Paul II, 1998, No. 8).

When Wojtyla speaks of the person, through the process of education, coming to apprehend the truth, it is important to remember that he views individuals' knowledge of this truth as integrally bound up with their own subjective knowledge and experience. For this reason it is important to keep in mind that the "subject-less" objective truth does not exist. Even the most objective of truths resides within a subjective person, God himself, as was indicated above. This being the case, all truth is, in a certain sense, subjective since it is really only persons who are able to know truth through their own existence. The term subjective, for Wojtyla, signifies more than the common philosophical meaning. When speaking of something as subjective, one should see it as being interiorized by the person, having meaning for the person within the context of that person's experience. Wojtyla writes,

Consciousness, insofar as it undoubtedly reflects whatever is objectified cognitively by the human being, at the same time and above all endows this objectified content with the subjective dimension proper to the human being as a subject. Consciousness interiorizes all that the human being cognizes, including everything that the individual cognizes from within in acts of self-knowledge, and makes it all a content of the subject's lived experience. (Wojtyla, 1993, p. 227)

This indicates that, for Wojtyla, education itself must take into account the individual's experience and perspective in order to be effective. It should also be noted that Wojtyla is able to maintain the existence of an universal objective truth common to all human persons by indicating that all human persons are called to an interactive relationship with God and therefore are able to come to an objective knowledge of things as they are in themselves.

Process of Education

Even though Wojtyla himself was a professional educator, at the university level, for the greater part of his ministry in Poland, he did not produce any sort of educational treatise explaining how one should go about the education of the human person. His methodology as a professor was traditional in that he taught by lecture, yet very untraditional in that he saw the educational process to be larger than could be contained in the four walls of a classroom or lecture hall. For most of his university ministry, he would lead groups of students on outings into the Polish countryside where he would continue his work as teacher; not necessarily covering material from a class syllabus, but by his conversation and example (Kwitny, 1997). There is no manner in which it is possible to categorize Wojtyla's pedagogical methodology, except to say that he sought to awaken in young persons all that was necessary for their self-education and self-fulfillment.

It is possible to arrive at some approximation of Wojtyla's pedagogical methodology by examining what he calls upon schools to do in order to fulfill the purpose of education. He writes that schools are called to,

cultivate in students the intellectual, creative and esthetic faculties of the individual; to develop in students the ability to make correct use of their judgment, will and affectivity; to promote in them a sense of values; to encourage just attitudes and prudent behavior; to introduce to them the cultural patrimony handed down from previous generations; to prepare them for their working lives

and to encourage the friendly interchange among students of diverse cultures and
backgrounds that will lead to mutual understanding and love. (Wojtyla/John Paul
II, 1987b, p. 154)

In order to accomplish all of this it becomes evident that the educator and
the school must involve the students in much more than the four walls of a
classroom and the retention of disparate facts. Education is an all
encompassing event in a person's life and needs to go beyond just the
classroom.

Wojtyla also sees the need to speak to students in light of the various
cultures and situations in which they are living. In speaking about
educating young people in the faith, he notes that, "genuine catechists
know that catechesis 'takes flesh' in the various cultures and milieu" and
that "to take, with wise discernment, certain elements, religious or
otherwise, that form part of the cultural heritage of a human group and use
them to help its members to understand better the whole of the Christian
mystery" (Wojtyla/John Paul II, 1979b, No. 53). There is little doubt that
what may be useful, indeed necessary, for the teaching of the faith, is
equally as useful or necessary for the teaching of any academic subject.
Being able to speak to students in a language they understand and in
reference to their everyday life experience is part of Wojtyla's educational
process (Wojtyla/John Paul II, 1979b, Nos. 40 and 49). It must also be
pointed out that Wojtyla would call for the viewing of each culture of
humankind to be placed in right relation to the truth. A cultural element
may be contrary to what is objectively "right" and therefore it must be held
up as not befitting the human person.

While culture is to be viewed as a medium for the education of the
student, it cannot be held up to the student as a boundary which encloses
and limits the person. Culture is that into which a person is born, but it is
also something which is created by the person or persons living within that
culture. Wojtyla writes that culture is created by the actions of persons,

to the extent that we do not become slaves of activity and of accomplishing
various works, but experience wonder and awe at reality..., to the extent that we
attain within ourselves a strong sense of the cosmos, a strong sense of the order
of the world, both the macro- and the microcosm, and make them a dominant
feature of our understanding, rather than merely a grand, but somehow also
brutal, instrument of our exploitation. (Wojtyla, 1993, p. 270)

The involvement of the person in this process of learning through culture as well as constructing culture emphasizes once again the importance of the person's ability to be free to act toward self-fulfillment.

In addition to making use of the culture of the student, Wojtyla points out that catechesis, and by extension, all education, must continually seek new methods in order to carry out its purpose. He holds that there needs to be a willingness to try new approaches and at the same time a sensible evaluation of any novelty. Wojtyla writes that,

> catechesis needs to be continually renewed by a certain broadening of its concept, by the revision of its methods, by the search for suitable language, and by the utilization of new means of transmitting the message...It is important for the Church to give proof today...of evangelical wisdom, courage and fidelity in seeking out and putting into operation new methods and new prospects for catechetical instruction. (Wojtyla/John Paul II, 1979b, No. 17)

There is a continual call, on Wojtyla's part, to maintain a sense of balance when approaching the educational enterprise. This balance will, in the long run, allow for the best possible experience for the students. The obvious danger, which he cautions against, is remaining content with the *status quo,* thinking that what has always worked well will continue to work, whether well, or at all.

Wojtyla does maintain, when speaking of catechesis in particular, that within education there is a need for the retention of fact and information and that this can often take the form of memorization. He notes that in secular education,

> more and more complaints are being made about the unfortunate consequences of disregarding the human faculty of memory, should we not attempt to put this faculty back into use in an intelligent and even an original way in catechesis?...A certain memorization...far from being opposed to the dignity of young Christians...is a real need. (Wojtyla/John Paul II, 1979b, No. 55)

It is interesting to note that Wojtyla makes specific reference to the possibility that memorization could lead to a lowering of the dignity of the young person. Although he dismisses this as not the case, his concern that it may reiterates the continuing theme of all his discussions on education: the true self-fulfillment of the human person and the avoidance of anything that impedes this process. This concern leads to his reminding teachers that, while memory is important, it is essential that "the texts that

are memorized must at the same time be taken in and gradually understood in depth, in order to become a source of Christian life on the
personal level and the community level" (Wojtyla/John Paul II, 1979b,
No. 55).

Wojtyla's approach indicates once again the importance of self-
integration: the person must be enabled to continually relate factual
knowledge with his own life and experience. The ability to relate facts does
not indicate that the person has been able to integrate that knowledge into
himself by the processes of horizontal and vertical transcendence. This is
accomplished, by the ability of the person to connect these facts or truths
to personal experience. It is personal experience which enables the person
to make knowledge real in his or her own life. Wojtyla writes that,

> the truths studied in catechesis are the same truths that touched the person's
> heart when he heard them for the first time. Far from blunting or exhausting
> them, the fact of knowing them better should make them even more challenging
> and decisive for one's life. (Wojtyla/John Paul II, 1979b, No. 25)

Although once again speaking specifically about catechesis, his point can
properly be extended to include all education. Because something sparked
interest in persons in the first place, they are able to make that something a
part of their lives by learning more about it. The learning all about the fact
does not make it part of the person, but rather the experience of the fact
makes it something which the person desires to know more about. Simply
put, education, whether in the faith or in secular subjects, cannot be just
on the level of abstract formulae, it must be tied to life experience, and by
so doing, add meaning and clarity to the person's life.

What has been seen in this examination of the educative process, is
that Wojtyla does not necessarily adhere to any single method. Rather, he
attempts to bring to educators (whether parents or school teachers) the
idea that any method which has, as its basis, the desire to bring the student
to self-fulfillment should be used. The antithesis to this statement is also
true: a method of education which does not first seek to assist the student
in the process of self-fulfillment should be rejected as not worthy of the
human person. Wojtyla (1993) writes that,

> This once again confirms the thesis that the basis of the process of education
> should be sought more deeply than in certain types of activities and endeavors,
> that ultimately what is at issue here is the bestowal of mature humanity upon
> those to whom the parents have given human life...Anything opposed to this,

even in areas seemingly removed from the direct educational process, must also have adverse educational effects. (p. 335)

Another way in which this point is brought to the fore is in Wojtyla's emphasis on the individual person's experience playing an important role in his education. Education, by its very nature, must always relate to where a person is, in his very self, in order to have any effect whatsoever. Because education exists to assist the person in personal development, this education must permeate every aspect of the person's life.

> Education is not reducible to a set or system of activities, but through them it reaches to a more basic reality, to a whole 'system of being.' Education then takes place more through who and what one is than through the different educational endeavors themselves in separation from this basis. (Wojtyla, 1993, p. 334)

This view of education places a great deal of pressure upon the teacher to relate to the student as a person, to enter into community with each student, so as to be able to be effective in the work of education. The necessity of establishing community for education to occur will be discussed at length later, suffice it to say now that, for Wojtyla, the teacher must be more than just a purveyor of information. What the teacher must be for the student will be discussed below.

The Role of Teachers and Parents

Although Wojtyla views the educational process as an active one on the part of the learner, he does not understand the teacher, as was mentioned above to be a mere passive entity in the enterprise. In keeping with his understanding of how human persons are able to communicate knowledge of things, in general, and of other persons, in particular, Wojtyla sees the teacher as an important part of the educative process. As was seen in Chapter III, the person can be known and can come to know others through the performance of a human act. In light of this, Wojtyla sees the teacher not so much as one who teaches through just the spoken word, although this too has its role, but predominantly through who they are as a person. The student learns by observing the words, deeds, emotions, etc., of the teacher: in short, through the teacher's entire person.

Since it is teachers who, through their own actions, reveal who they are as persons to the student, they are able to assist the students in the process of transcendence, and thus self-fulfillment. Teachers, and, because they are the natural teachers of their children, parents as well, form an integral part in leading their charges by example from their own lives. It is for this reason that Wojtyla understands the need for parents and teachers to be progressing along the road to self-fulfillment themselves. The Scholastic axiom "you cannot give what you do not have" would more than adequately reflect Wojtyla's understanding of the teacher's role.

It is possible to see another dimension to Wojtyla's view of the teacher when he speaks, not just from his philosophical approach but also from his theological, of Jesus as the Teacher. Here again is faced the challenge of moving with Wojtyla from being the philosopher to being the theologian and authoritative teacher. But, as before, by moving with him, a fuller understanding of his philosophical meaning is obtained. Just as Jesus, as a person, shows the human person what it means to be fully self-fulfilled, so too Jesus' life as a teacher is a model for all teachers to follow. Wojtyla, in speaking of the vocation of the teacher, notes that

> Jesus taught in word and deed, and his teaching cannot be separated from his life and being. In the Apostolic Exhortation on Catechesis I stated: "The whole of Christ's life was a continual teaching: his silences, his miracles, his gestures, his prayer, his love for people, his special affection for the poor, his acceptance of the total sacrifice on the cross for the redemption of the world and his resurrection..." Dear friends: Jesus shares with you his teaching ministry. (Wojtyla/John Paul II, 1987b, p. 155)

Just as Jesus taught by every act that he performed and by every word he spoke, so, too, does the teacher.

By having this understanding of the manner in which teachers goes about their vocation, Wojtyla is, in a sense, placing an added burden on the teacher; not only must the correct information be taught, but also the truly human way of acting must be presented to the student. This requires that teachers be persons who continually model to their students the process of self-fulfillment through transcendence, integration, and self-education. When the role of teacher is seen in this way, it is much clearer why Wojtyla uses the image of the crucifix as the model of Christ the teacher: the work of teacher is one of continual self-sacrifice (transcendence) in order to help the student understand what self-fulfillment is all about. In order to bring about the end of education which he puts forward, Wojtyla envisions the teacher as one who personally shows the student how to move toward self-fulfillment. The words Wojtyla uses to describe Christ the teacher can rightly, in his estimation, be applied to any teacher. Just as Jesus is a teacher who "saves, forgives, sanctifies and guides, who lives, who speaks, rouses, moves, redresses, judges, forgives, and goes with us day by day on the path of history," (Wojtyla/John Paul II, 1979b, No. 9) so must the teacher of others be. The teacher is therefore one who is continually involved with every aspect of one's students' lives. In short, one who loves one's students as Christ loves them.

Because of this extremely demanding view of what it means to be teacher, Wojtyla does not speak about the teaching "occupation", but rather the teaching "vocation." Persons do not become teachers because they are in need of a source of income, but rather because they are called to it; called to a vocation in which they accept both its rewards and sacrifices, its joys and sorrows. Since Wojtyla views this vocation as coming from Jesus, he reminds teachers that it is only in their relationship with Jesus that they will be able to be faithful to their role. He writes that,

> Only in close communion with him [Jesus] can you respond adequately. This is my hope, this is my prayer; that you will be totally open to Christ. That he will give you an ever greater love for your students and an ever stronger commitment to your vocation as Catholic educators. If you continue to be faithful to this ministry today as you have been in the past, you will be doing much in shaping a peaceful, just and hope-filled world for the future. (Wojtyla/John Paul II, 1987b, p. 155)

In presenting the vocation of teacher in this light, Wojtyla is once again calling upon his own experience as teacher. His singular devotion to, and love of, his students, as well as his being a part of their lives, has been recognized as the source of his effectiveness as a teacher. Mieczyslaw Malinski noted this quality of Wojtyla the teacher. He writes,

> What was true of his young friends in Krakow was also true of his students in Lublin. He and they were a group of friends, engaged with all their hearts and minds in studying problems in which they were deeply interested. They were a family united not only by lectures and seminars but by daily life together: the affairs of one were the affairs of all, and members of the group would help and support one another in everything. (Malinski, 1979, p. 138)

The use of the term *friend* to describe Wojtyla's relationship with his students would seem to imply that there was a level of familiarity which would impede his ability to be teacher, especially when the teacher would have to correct. Malinski also notes that there was a lack of formality in the relationship between Wojtyla and his students but that this did not diminish the respect the young people had for their teacher. Malinski (1979) states that,

> Karol's [Wojtyla's] young companions called him 'Wujek' ('uncle'): there was no vestige of formality, and the whole atmosphere was one of comradeship. It seems strange today when one attempts to describe it—words, no doubt, are inadequate to any reality, and especially so when the reality is something new and unusual. For all their frankness and simplicity of the young people's behavior, they genuinely respected their 'uncle.' (p. 108)

What it is important to realize is that Wojtyla's understanding of the teaching vocation comes not only from his theoretical knowledge, but also from his lived experience as an educator.

Although Wojtyla does present a very spiritualized understanding of the vocation of an educator, he is also cognizant of the need for all educators to be men and women who are knowledgeable in their academic discipline as well as pedagogical methodology. He notes that educators must "be constantly challenged by high professional standards in preparing and teaching their courses" (Wojtyla/John Paul II, 1987b, p. 154). These high professional standards are required in order to help the educator to become a better teacher; they cannot, in themselves, guarantee the successfulness of the teacher.

As was discussed above, the educational process, from Wojtyla's perspective, is a reciprocal one; the students learn from the teacher while, at the same time, the teacher learns from the students. This obviously necessitates that the teacher be open to the process of learning from his students. Wojtyla, even in his later life, has noted that he himself seeks to learn from the young people he comes in contact with. He writes that, whenever he meets with young people, he waits,

> first of all to hear what they want to tell me about themselves, about their society, about their Church. And I always point out: 'What I am going to say to you is not as important as what you are going to say to me. You will not necessarily say it to me in words; you will say it to me by your presence, by your song, perhaps by your dancing, by your skits, and finally by your enthusiasm. (Wojtyla/John Paul II, 1994c, pp. 124-125)

This willingness to learn from students also implies that the teacher have a profound respect for the students as persons. If each student is seen as a person, then it becomes obvious, based upon Wojtyla's understanding, that any interaction between teacher and student is an opportunity for an "I"-"Thou" relationship and horizontal transcendence. It is this respect for the personhood of the students which ultimately leads the teacher to the love of the students. In cases where teachers have ceased to have respect for the personhood of their students, and by extension, have ceased to love them, their role as teacher is seriously compromised.

When discussing the role of the teacher in Wojtyla's educational thought, it is impossible to ignore the importance of the parents of the students. For Wojtyla, the parents of the child are its first and primary teachers, a role which they must take seriously and a right which may not, unless there is serious harm possible to the child, be taken from them. In his Apostolic Exhortation, *Familiaris Consortio*, Wojtyla writes,

> The right and duty of parents to give education is essential, since it is connected with the transmission of human life; it is original and primary with regard to the educational role of others, on account of the uniqueness of the loving relationship between parents and children; and it is irreplaceable and inalienable, and therefore incapable of being entirely delegated to others or usurped by others. (Wojtyla/John Paul II, 1981a, No. 36)

This picture of the role of the parent which is painted by Wojtyla is very much in keeping with the traditional educational teaching of the Church: all of the official Church documents dealing with education, as presented above, speak of the parents' role as being essential and absolute. Wojtyla's addition to the thought is his presentation of love being the most significant part of the role of the parents in education. This love is what enables the child, and later, the young person, to move along the path of life toward self-fulfillment.

Additionally, it is the teacher's role to educate the young person by loving him or her, as well; in this manner Wojtyla shows how the teacher's role is sharing in the work of the parents in the education of their children. Since the parent and the teacher share the responsibility of bringing the young person to self-fulfillment, there should be a clear involvement of the parent in the work of the teacher in the school. Wojtyla noted to Catholic school teachers that, "as educators you correctly see your role as cooperating with parents in their primary responsibility. Your efforts to involve them in the whole educational process are commendable" (Wojtyla/John Paul II, 1987b, p. 154). While this emphasis on the role of parents is important, Wojtyla also recognizes how much more important the role of the teacher becomes when dealing with the current sociological phenomena of the single parent home. The work of the Catholic school teacher becomes even "more urgent for those young ones who come from broken homes and who, often with only one parent to encourage them, must draw support and direction from their teachers in school" (Wojtyla/John Paul II, 1987b, p. 155).

Wojtyla has significantly more to say about the role of parents in the education of their child, but, for the most part, this is presented within his discussion of the family as a community. For this reason, the remaining elements of his thought regarding the role of parents will be presented in Chapter V which deals specifically with the role of community in the education of the person.

Quite obviously, no philosophy of education would be complete without devoting a substantial amount of thought to the role of the student in the entire enterprise. Wojtyla, given his own life experience as an educator, has devoted a significant amount of his writing to coming to an understanding of the education (i.e., growing toward self-fulfillment) of the young person. For this reason, his view of the role of the student will be discussed in an extended fashion in Chapter VI, in order to give it the attention it clearly merits in Wojtyla's view of education. What is important to take away from this overview of Wojtyla's thought on the education of the human person is that he clearly understands the student's role to be one of active participation. Indeed, it should be recalled that he has often referred to the education of the young person as being self-education. How this concept plays itself out in his overall philosophy of education will be taken up below, in Chapter V.

Questions Concerning Wojtyla's Educational Philosophy

Theory or Practical Application? Before moving on to consider the role of community in the education of the human person, there are some areas in which further clarification from Wojtyla's point of view would prove helpful. The first of these questions involves the practical application of

Wojtyla's extremely philosophical approach to education. It could well be asked if his thoughts on this entire topic are simply too theoretical to be of any real benefit to furthering the formation of a Catholic philosophy of education.

Obviously, as written, Wojtyla's educational ideas are very theoretical, which, in and of itself, is not a bad thing. In any enterprise, concrete practice needs to have some theoretical base. The more important question is how Wojtyla himself would view his writings on education: is he providing the theoretical base, or is he providing what, in his estimation, is a blueprint for the practice of education? If his attempt has been to give a blueprint, then he has not succeeded; there are too many ideas without concrete structure. If his attempt has been to provide theory, then he has been able to do just that. Discovering his intent, then, becomes the real issue.

Throughout Wojtyla's voluminous writings, one seemingly innocuous, statement stands out. This statement gives a clear hint of what he himself regards as the source of his writing and how he intends his writings to be viewed. In recalling the gargantuan effort he had to put forward when he first began his philosophical studies, Wojtyla tells Andre Frossard (1984) that,

> After two months of hacking through this vegetation [philosophy] I came to a clearing, to the discovery of the deep reasons for what until then I had only lived and felt...What intuition and sensibility had until then taught me about the world found solid confirmation...Books, study, reflection and discussion—which I do not avoid, as you know—help me to formulate what experience teaches me. (pp. 17–18)

From Wojtyla's own words come the realization that he is writing theory, theory which he has formulated based upon his own practical experience of life. It would be safe to say that Wojtyla intends his work to be taken in just that light: theory which may, or may not, assist practitioners in understanding the "why" behind what they do based upon experience.

What of Academic Freedom in the Search for Truth? With the publication of *Ex Corde Ecclesiae*, *Veritatis Splendor* and *Fides et Ratio*, the concern has been voiced that Wojtyla is seeking to put a curb on academic "free speech," for lack of a better term, especially among

Catholic theologians and philosophers. Since Wojtyla has tried to effecttively silence the voice of some educators through these documents, it can
well be asked if his understanding of education (being self-fulfillment
through the search for truth) is nothing more than theoretical nonsense
which he obviously does not follow himself.

Some have questioned whether Wojtyla sees truth as the desired goal
or if his desire for doctrinal orthodoxy has superceded truth as the end to
intellectual pursuits. Bernard Haring envisions an even more ignoble
intent on Wojtyla's part when he writes, commenting on *Veritatis Splendor*, that,

> His [Wojtyla's] starting point is a high sense of duty, combined with absolute
> trust in his own competence, with the special assistance of the Holy Spirit. And
> this absolute trust in his own powers is coupled with a profound distrust toward
> all theologians (particularly moral theologians) who might not be in total sym-
> pathy with him. (Haring, 1994, p. 10)

Haring's initial point regarding Wojtyla's approach in *Ex Corde Ecclesiae*
probably best defines the issue: Wojtyla's sense of duty regarding his role
as Pope clearly influences the tone and intent with which he limits
academic freedom.

It is in discussing this issue that the real conflict between Wojtyla the
philosopher and Wojtyla the authoritative teacher comes to the fore.
While almost every element of Wojtyla's philosophy would lead to the
belief that he would be a strong advocate of a liberal application of the
concept of academic freedom, this is not carried forward in Wojtyla's
words and actions as pope. Wojtyla's own intellectual freedom has, in a
sense, had limits placed upon it as well. Although it is often assumed that
the reigning pope has unlimited power and authority, there are certainly
defining boundaries placed upon him. George Weigel (1999) notes that
these limits were made clear by the Second Vatican Council's
"Theological Commission which noted that 'the Roman Pontiff is also
bound to revelation itself, to the fundamental structure of the Church, to
the sacraments, to the definitions of earlier Councils, and other obligations
too numerous to mention'" (p. 264). Wojtyla clearly understands the limits
placed upon his authority and intellectual pursuits. He, as well,
understands that as pope, he "is the custodian of an *authoritative* tradition
of teaching, a 'magisterium,' that defines the boundaries of the Church"

and that, as pope, he "is its [the magisterium's] servant, not its master" (Weigel, 1999, p. 264).

Given Wojtyla's approach toward his own university professorial colleagues and their investigations, not to mention his own, it would appear that *Ex Corde Ecclesiae*'s discussion of academic freedom is not a full reflection of the mind of Wojtyla the philosopher. It is clearly a document coming out of Wojtyla's need to "do his duty" as authoritative teacher. While it may be very difficult to discern what Wojtyla the philosopher would expound as the meaning of academic freedom in relation to the search for truth, it would be unfair to condemn the philosopher as being inconsistent since it is not the philosopher who is speaking in *Ex Corde Ecclesiae*. Wojtyla the philosopher's thought regarding academic freedom is, therefore, one which will never be adequately known and any contradictions between elements of his philosophy and *Ex Corde Ecclesiae* must remain unresolved.

Now that Wojtyla's overall understanding of the educative process has been presented, it is possible to move on to the work of examining, in depth, two important issues which were only touched on above: the role of community in education and the role of the young person in education.

V

COMMUNITY AND EDUCATION

Up to this point, the examination of Wojtyla's work has been centered primarily upon the educational process and the individual person. It has been shown that Wojtyla views education as the process whereby a person is able to embark upon the life-long process of self-fulfillment through transcendence and integration. When Wojtyla's overall philosophical anthropology was examined, it became obvious that, in his thought, the individual person is only able to come to self-fulfillment by being in community with other persons. In fact, for Wojtyla, one cannot speak about fulfilling oneself as a person without speaking of going out of the self and giving of self to the community (Wojtyla, 1993, pp. 246–252).

The intrinsic nature of community in the process of self-fulfillment in the individual person clearly necessitates investigating what role and function the community has in the educative process. It is to this task that this chapter is dedicated. The role of community will be examined by first looking, at how Wojtyla's philosophical themes of community, participation, and solidarity relate to his philosophical understanding of the human person. Following this, three specific embodiments of community which are pertinent, for Wojtyla, when speaking of education, will be investigated: the family, the school, and the larger human society. Additionally, the manner in which individual persons are able to be part of these communities will be examined. Specifically this will entail studying the roles which participation and alienation play in the process of education and the forming of true communities in the family, in the school, and in society-at-large. Flowing from this look into participation and alienation will be the issue of solidarity and its importance in the educational enterprise. With this basic outline of this chapter in place, it is now possible to examine the philosophical themes of community, solidarity, and participation.

Philosophical Themes: Community, Solidarity, and Participation

As was referred to above, the personalist philosopher is always attempting to maintain the balance between the person and the person-in-community and Wojtyla is no exception. Although *The Acting Person* concerns itself ostensibly with coming to an understanding of the individual person, Wojtyla concludes his work with a rather lengthy exposition on the relationship between the individual person and the community. In addition to this concluding section in *The Acting Person*, he has written extensively on this same topic. What follows is an attempt to present a synthesis of his understanding of the person-in-community as well as how this understanding gives rise to two other themes given prominence in his work, solidarity and participation.

Wojtyla begins his discussion concerning the person-in-community by indicating that it is only in relation to another person that a person is able to establish what it means to be an "I." My consciousness of myself as an individual person comes into full relief only when "I" am somehow in relation with "Thou." Additionally, this relationship establishes the identity of the "Thou" as another subjective person. The "Thou" is related to differently than a rock or a chair because the "I" recognizes in the "Thou" a being like itself. Along with this experience comes the understanding that the "I" is also a "Thou" when in relation to another "I." The person in relation to another person thus simultaneously experiences oneself as both the subject of one's own experience and the object of another person's experience. All of this is presented by Wojtyla to underscore the importance of other persons in even the most basic of human experiences: being the subject of my own consciousness. It is also in this presentation of the "I"-"Thou" relationship that the influence of Martin Buber can be seen most clearly (Buber, 1996, pp. 111–119).

Having established the importance of the "I"-"Thou" relationship, Wojtyla proceeds to explain the difference between merely being in an "I"-"Thou" relationship and being in community with other persons. By sensing the presence of a "Thou," the "I" is able to establish his subjectness. The establishment of community implies the presence of "I"-"Thou" relationships

in which human beings mutually reveal themselves to one another in their personal human subjectivity and in all that goes to make up this subjectivity. The "thou" stands before my self as a true and complete "other self," which, like my own self, is characterized not only by self determination, but also and above all by self-possession and self-governance. (Wojtyla, 1993, p. 245)

A community is established, then, where there is horizontal transcendence occurring between two persons. This community can come into existence between two or more persons. Given the place the community of persons holds in the establishment of horizontal transcendence, it is also important to note that the community is a source of growth toward the self-fulfillment of the individual person. Also, as the community assists the person in self-fulfillment, the person is able to give back more of oneself to the community. In a true community, therefore, the individual and the community are continually enriching one another. This being the case, being part of a community of persons is not an option for the individual person; personhood means being in community with other persons.

The entire process by which the individual person enters into a relationship with any community is based upon the ability of the person to give oneself as gift to another person. In fact, it is only by this gift of self that the individual person is able to find self-fulfillment and to be enriched by being in community. Wojtyla (1993) writes,

> In the communal relationship that occurs between persons, this self fulfillment is realized through the mutual gift of self, a gift that has a disinterested character... In interhuman relationships, therefore, the disinterested gift of self (of the person) stands at the basis of the whole order of love and the whole authenticity of love. (p. 322)

This willingness, on the part of the individual person, to give of self is what makes real community possible in the first place. When the person gives of self without looking for what one will get in return, i.e., disinterestedly, the person is able to move towards horizontal as well as vertical transcendence. The obvious antithesis to this gift of self to the community is selfishness. A person who acts in a manner that indicates he is only concerned with himself, is a person who is not part of a community, a person who is not transcending self and therefore not moving toward integration and self-fulfillment.

While it would appear that all that is necessary for the community's formation and functioning is the movement of all members toward self-donation, this is not the case. Wojtyla is clear on the need for the community to be accepting of the gift offered. He writes that, in order for interpersonal relationships to be authentic, there must be a

> genuine reception of the gift or of the act through which the gift of the person is expressed. One may not divorce the person from the gift he or she brings; one may not strip away from this giving of self who the person truly is and what the person truly intends to express by his or her activity. (Wojtyla, 1993, p. 322)

This theme of self-gift, or self-donation, reappears frequently in Wojtyla's writings on education and will therefore be an important point to examine in regard to the education of the person.

Since all persons ought to be, by their very nature as persons, members of a community, Wojtyla moves on to speak about participation. As was noted above, just being aware of the presence of another person does not establish the horizontal transcendence which is the hallmark of a community of persons. The concept of participation is put forward to indicate the freedom a person has to have to be involved in a community, the gift of self the person is called to make to the community, and also the need for this gift to be accepted by the community. Participation occurs when the person has the ability to freely act together with other persons in such a way as to remain fully self-possessed and able to move toward greater self-fulfillment, through the gift of self. This means that a person can be said to be in a community only in so far as the person is able to participate. Participation assures the continuing cycle of community helping to fulfill the person and the person helping the community to fulfill itself.

Wojtyla is quick to point out that being able to participate is not just the responsibility of the individual person, but also of the community at large. A community which does not work towards having full participation by all members must change so as to allow the participation of all members (Wojtyla, 1993, pp. 202–203). When a person is unable to participate in the community, the person endures alienation. Alienation prevents the person from acting freely, thus preventing one's self-possession and self-fulfillment. Just as participation allows for the continued fulfillment of both the person and the community, alienation diminishes both the person and the community. Alienation is, therefore, a condition which is not worthy of the human person and must be overcome.

Up to this point, the discussion of community has been revolving around the "I"-"Thou" relationship. Additionally, Wojtyla notes that human experience is also aware of the relationship that is in existence when the word "we" is used. "We" connotes the sense of unity which is experienced by a community of persons who are engaged in working toward a common good for the entire community. When the entire community ("we") is engaged in pursuit of the realization of this common good for all members of the community, solidarity can be said to exist. Wojtyla (1979a) defines solidarity as,

> the attitude of a community, in which the common good properly conditions and initiates participation, and participation in turn properly serves the common good, fosters it, and furthers its realization. 'Solidarity' means the constant readiness to accept and to realize one's share in the community because of one's membership within that particular community. (pp. 284–285)

Clearly, solidarity is what every community of persons is to be about.

With this understanding of the role of community in the development of the human person, it is now possible to look at the three specific instances of human community which are pertinent to education: the family, the school, and human society.

The Community of the Family

When one begins to sift through the vast quantities of Wojtyla's written works and public allocutions, an issue takes on a centrality which may not be completely expected. That issue is the family. The first of his books, *Love and Responsibility*, was written, in 1960, as a guide for the preparation of young people for marriage and the establishment of their own families. The first of his thematic allocutions as pope, given during the Wednesday public audiences, was concerned with the exegesis of the creation stories in the beginning of the book of Genesis and how these showed God's plan for the establishment of the family. The first Synod of Bishops over which Wojtyla presided as pope, concerned itself with the family and resulted in his Apostolic Exhortation, *Familiaris Consortio.*

Study of and concern for the family as a community of persons united in love provides the impetus for all Wojtyla's philosophical reflections as well. Malinski, reflecting on the origins of Wojtyla's interests and writings, notes that,

> Above all he was interested in the supreme experience which is love—both love
> in general, if one may put it so, and particular forms of it such as married love...
> He was able to see how feelings of attraction gradually developed into love; he
> was there when couples took the decision to marry and start a new kind of
> existence, and when their lives were again transformed by the advent of children.
> (Malinski, 1979, p. 138)

It is clear that Wojtyla's interest and writing concerning the family is not
solely based upon the traditional teaching of the Church. In his mind, the
family is the first step toward the realization of the goal of education, the
fulfillment of the human person. How this is so is the beginning of coming
to terms with the role of the family in the educative process.

The Origin of the Family Community. The family, as Wojtyla
understands it, arises from the freely chosen act of self-giving of a man and
a woman, who, by virtue of this gift, one to another, form a community of
persons (Wojtyla, 1993, p. 318). This community, Wojtyla reminds his
readers,

> does not just refer to something in common, to community as a certain effect or
> even expression of the being and acting of person. It refers rather to the very
> mode of being and acting of those persons, which is a mode of being and acting
> in mutual relation to one another (not just "in common" with one another) such
> that through this being and acting they mutually confirm and affirm one another
> as persons. (Wojtyla, 1993, p. 321)

The community established by husband and wife is reflective of the
community spoken of above whereby human persons are able to freely act
so as to move toward horizontal transcendence. It is in light of this reality
that the family takes on its central role in society, although this societal role
is only secondary to the development of a community of persons. The act
of the giving of oneself, which brings each family into existence, is what
moves the persons involved toward self-fulfillment. Wojtyla (1993) writes
that,

> Self-fulfillment is realized through the mutual gift of self, a gift that has a
> disinterested character...If it were to serve some "interest" on one side or the
> other, it would no longer be a gift. It might perhaps be beneficial and even
> useful, but it would not be gratuitous...Personal development takes place through
> the disinterested gift of self. (p. 322)

The self-fulfillment which ought to come about through this mutual gift of self also implies that the gift is accepted by both the man and the woman. The inability or decision not to accept what the other person is offering stifles the ongoing self-fulfillment of the spouses and impedes the development of a true community of persons.

The community of persons which is established by the marriage of a man and a woman takes on a new reality when the man and the woman become father and mother. Wojtyla (1993) notes that, "there can be no doubt that the state of parenthood in the man as father and the woman as mother objectively produces a new dimension, a new qualification, in their personal and social life" (p. 330). The birth of a child, in a very real way, reemphasizes the communal nature of the relationship between the man and woman. The pair can only define themselves as father and mother in relation to the other. Wojtyla (1993) explains that,

> The very essence of this social and communal system (this *communio personarum*) lies in the fact that the man's fatherhood always occurs through the woman's motherhood and, vice versa, the woman's motherhood through the man's fatherhood. This is an internally closed and objectively necessary system. Parenthood needs to be affirmed in a special way on the basis of the *communio personarum*. (p. 330)

When woman and man see in their respective new titles of "mother" and "father" the reality of their gift to each other, their community is strengthened and the new community formed with the birth of their child will be in good stead to be life giving to each member.

An additional point which Wojtyla makes regarding the community of the family is its mirroring the image of God. The Scriptures continually speak of the human person as being made in the image and likeness of God. Wojtyla points out, following Thomas Aquinas, that this image of God is reflected in a meaningful way in the fact that human beings need to be, by nature, in community with other human beings. Because God is, by nature, a community of three divine persons, so God's image is reflected when human persons create communities. Besides reflecting God's communal nature in the community of persons formed through marriage, man and woman further reflect God's image when, through their free gift of selves, they create a new human person to be in community with them (Wojtyla, 1993, p. 318). Thus, the conception and birth of a child is infinitely more than mere biological reproduction of the species, but an actual sharing in the creative action of God (Wojtyla/John Paul II, 1994b, No. 7). There is, therefore, a profound meaning to the conception and birth of a child which brings with it responsibilities; most particularly, the education of the child. With the understanding that the conception and birth of the child involves the cooperative action between the parents and God, comes the realization that the child is not the property of its mother and father. It is a human person who now enters into this familial community and, in so doing, begins the process of horizontal transcendence for both itself and its parents (Wojtyla, 1993, p. 333).

The Educative Role of the Family Community. By being the community that it is, the family is the first place in which the child will come to see himself as a person. As was presented above, it is only when an "I" is able to be in relation with a "Thou" that the individual personhood of the human being is defined. The first of these "I"-"Thou" relationships which the child experiences is within the family community as it begins to relate to its parents as mother and father and to its siblings in a similar fashion. From the first moment, then, of the child's introduction into the family community, the process of education has begun. This is the case because the first step in becoming a fulfilled human person involves the recognition that the person is an "I" that is not a "Thou." The process of education, thus begun, continues as the child matures in its personhood and is able to see the giving of self, which is so essential to self-fulfillment, exemplified in its parents and siblings. Wojtyla presents this concept when he tries to point out that for parents, educating their child can be said stated simply as the,

> making a gift of mature humanity to this little person, this gradually developing human being. One could say that, from the perspective of the communal structure of the family, childhood signifies the passive need for such giving, and parenthood, the active potentiality—the readiness and capacity—for such giving. (Wojtyla, 1993, p. 334)

The educative role of the family, then, is in providing a community where the example of what it means to be a self-fulfilled human person (a person able to experience horizontal and vertical transcendence in relation to the truth, act in accord with this truth, and, in so doing, able to give of self to others) is exemplified. By its very nature this family community is one of continual self-giving, first by the parents and then, as they mature, on the part of the children. Wojtyla notes this when he writes that, "education then is before all else a reciprocal "offering" on the part of both parents: together they communicate their own mature humanity to the newborn child, who gives them in turn the newness and freshness of the humanity which it has brought into the world" (Wojtyla/John Paul II, 1994b, No. 16). Here is very clearly seen Wojtyla's view of what the educator (teacher) should be: the parents, as educators, teach more by the example of their lives than by any specific teaching they attempt to convey.

When speaking of the role of the family community, and most specifically regarding the role of parents, Wojtyla seems to present the concept that the role of children is passive in education. This presentation seems to be at odds with his emphasis upon the active role which children play in their education through the process of self-education. This contradiction, is, however, in appearance only. Wojtyla's comments should be understood to indicate that the process of education is never passive, whether one is speaking of the student or the educator. Thus, there is a continual process of give and take; student and educator both are co-workers in the educational enterprise.

What should be noted, having examined the role which the young person's "first" community has in education, is that Wojtyla views this role as integral to education. Without the presence of a true *communio personarum,* the process of education will not take place; a true educative community must be in place in order for the young person to achieve the proper end of education, self-fulfillment. This point is made clearly by Wojtyla when he writes,

> Education is thus a unique process for which the mutual communion of persons has immense importance. The educator is a person who "begets" in a spiritual sense...It is a living means of communication, which not only creates a profound relationship between the educator and the one being educated, but also makes them both sharers in truth and love, that final goal to which everyone is called by God the Father, Son and Holy Spirit. (Wojtyla/John Paul II, 1994b, No. 16)

Having established the need for the existence of a *communio person-arum* in order for education to take place, Wojtyla moves on to the need which parents have to involve others in the educational enterprise. Clearly echoing the role of parents as presented in *Divini Illius Magistri* (Pius XI, 1929) Wojtyla emphasizes the central and inalienable role which parents have regarding the education of their children. He does, however, introduces the principle of *subsidiarity* into the discussion. Subsidiarity is a concept used in the more recent writings of the Church which means that the persons closest to any given situation or task should be the ones to deal with it. Only in the case where certain elements are beyond the competency of the closest persons should others be involved in the situation. In the case of education, Wojtyla applies this principle to the family community: only when the family community is not able to fulfill its proper role should other communities, whether educational or political, become involved. He writes,

> Parents are the first and most important educators of their own children, and they also possess a fundamental competence in this area: They are educators because they are parents. They share their educational mission with other individuals or institutions such as the Church and the state. But the mission of education must always be carried out in accordance with a proper application of the principle of subsidiarity. (Wojtyla/John Paul II, 1994b, No. 16)

The need for parents to move outside the original family community in order to fulfill their responsibility to educate their children is evident enough and clearly recognized by Wojtyla. In addition to this, Wojtyla is equally strong in emphasizing the duty the political and ecclesial communities have toward assisting parents in their role as educators, as was Pius XI and the Second Vatican Council. He writes,

> The State and the Church have the obligation to give families all possible aid to enable them to perform their educational role properly. Therefore both the Church and the State must create and foster the institutions and activities that families justly demand, and the aid must be in proportion to the families' needs. (Wojtyla/John Paul II, 1981a, No. 40)

Having established the responsibilities of those outside the family to assist the family community in the education of the children, Wojtyla reminds parents that they, "have a serious duty to commit themselves totally to a cordial and active relationship with the teachers and the school authorities" (Wojtyla/John Paul II, 1981a, No. 40). What begins to emerge from Wojtyla's writings is a need for parents to become part of a larger community of education. The need for parents to become part of the larger school community is, "more necessary than ever, not to restrict the freedom of adolescents, but to mould it [adolescent freedom] and enable it to make responsible and well-motivated choices" (Wojtyla/John Paul II, 1997b, No. 2).

Thus far, Wojtyla has shown that the family community, being the first *communio personarum* to which a person belongs, is an essential element in the educational enterprise. Additionally, Wojtyla has indicated that the family community needs to associate other communities with itself in order to complete the process of education begun within the family. At this point it is possible to examine what role the school community, whether on the primary, secondary or post-secondary level, has to play in the education of the human person.

The Community of the School

As has been presented up to this point, the role of community in the full self-fulfillment of the human person, and therefore in education, is central in Wojtyla's thought. The person begins and continues his education within the context of the *communio personarum* of the family. This raises the question as to the role of the school within this process. Wojtyla has pointed out that parents are often in need of assistance when it comes to the education of their children, especially when it comes to specific academic disciplines and the proper socialization of the young persons. Does the school, therefore, in Wojtyla's thought, merely augment the community of the family with its specialties, or does it form a necessary *communio personarum* in its own right which is equally necessary for the education of the young persons who attend? It is the answer to this question which will be attempted here.

Before moving into the discussion of Wojtyla's understanding of the nature of the school community, it is important to note that Wojtyla makes his points concerning school community within the context of post-secondary education. This is not done to imply that the nature and importance of the school community is limited to university level, but rather because Wojtyla's personal experience comes from post-secondary education. Because of the value which he places upon personal experience in gaining understanding, he relies heavily upon his days as a university professor to present to his readers the integral part the school community plays in education.

The Nature of the School Community. There can be little doubt that, for Wojtyla, the school must form a true *communio personarum* in order for it to be a place of true education. This is evident from understanding the role which community plays in the self-fulfillment of the human person. The family community is the primal place of education by the fact that it is a community; its communal nature is what allows it to be a place of education. Wojtyla, therefore, being very much true to his overall understanding of education and the communities role in it, writes,

> A Catholic university pursues its objectives through its formation of an authentic human community animated by the spirit of Christ. It assists each of its members to achieve wholeness as human persons; in turn, everyone in the community helps in promoting unity, and each one, according to his or her role and capacity, contributes toward decisions which affect the community and also toward maintaining and strengthening the distinctive Catholic character of the institution. (Wojtyla/John Paul II, 1990a, No. 21)

Although this quote refers specifically to the university, it should be noted that the importance of the school being a community is applicable to all levels of education. Whether primary, secondary, post-secondary, or graduate level, the school must be a real community of all those engaged in the learning process. As was mentioned above, Wojtyla speaks of the university in particular because it is this which is central to his own experience.

As can be seen from Wojtyla's understanding of the university as a community, the school community possesses the same qualities necessary for the existence of a true *communio personarum*: a common goal, a respect for each person's contribution to the community and a desire to seek the truth and relate it to each person's life and the overall life of the community. To restate these qualities using Wojtyla's terminology: the school community must be a place which assists the person in horizontal and vertical transcendence, integration, self-education, and self-fulfillment, as well as allowing for full participation of all members of the community in a spirit of solidarity.

Formation of the School Community. This understanding of a school community is necessary for its success, but the work of actually creating such a community is difficult. In reflecting on the section of *Ex Corde*

Ecclesiae quoted above, Joseph Komonchak notes this difficulty and also, but more importantly, the value of such a community. After explaining that the educational community of the university seeks to be inclusive, respectful of all and formative of true scholarship, Komonchak (1993) states that, "the composite or mixture of disparate elements will not always be easy to maintain, but it is the realization of an ideal that is both humanely attractive and profoundly worthwhile" (p. 62).

Komonchak correctly identifies the difficulty in forming and worthiness of having such a school community but fails to note that, from Wojtyla's perspective, there really is no option. The school must form such a community if it is to be effective. When presenting his understanding of the family community, Wojtyla noted that there is a natural relationship between the members of a family and this natural relationship pre-establishes that community (Wojtyla, 1993, pp. 329–335). These natural relationships, by their very nature, are able to help the building of a true *communio personarum*. The school, on the other hand, will not, at the outset, have these natural relationships and therefore the work of building a true community of persons in the school is more complex.

Given the very real obstacles which need to be overcome in establishing a *communio personarum* within the school, Wojtyla notes that the responsibility of forming the community must be borne by all members, whether students, faculty, administration or staff. Relying upon his premise that all teaching is carried out through the example of the entire life of the teacher, Wojtyla calls upon teachers to,

> seek to improve their competence and endeavor to set the content, objectives, methods and results of research in an individual discipline within the framework of a coherent world vision. All teachers are to be inspired by academic ideals and by the principles of an authentically human life. (Wojtyla/John Paul II, 1990a, No. 22)

Thus, the contribution of the teachers to building the school community is their own personal examples of working towards being self-fulfilled human persons. This obviously necessitates having an understanding of education as being the assisting of students to become self-fulfilled. In addition, since the unifying force within the school must be the common task of seeking the truth (Wojtyla/John Paul II, 1990a, No. 21), teachers must always work towards presenting a unified understanding of truth by the integration of their various disciplines. It is in showing themselves to be seekers of the truth who willingly give of themselves to their students and other members of the school community in this endeavor that teachers contribute to the development of the community. Wojtyla notes the importance of the role which teachers can have in the development of the community of the school when he writes that,

> you are able, as Catholic educators, to introduce your students to a powerful experience of community and to a very serious involvement in social concerns that will enlarge their horizons, challenge their lifestyles and offer them authentic human fulfillment. (Wojtyla/John Paul II, 1987c, p. 163)

Wojtyla, in faithfulness to his understanding of education being, for the most part, self-education, maintains that the students have an integral role to play in the development and maintaining of the school community. In *Ex Corde Ecclesiae* he writes that,

> Students are challenged to pursue an education that combines excellence in humanistic and cultural development with specialized professional training. Most especially, they are challenged to continue the search for truth and for meaning throughout their lives. (Wojtyla/John Paul II, 1990a, No. 23)

Wojtyla is calling upon students to be active participants in the educational process: they are to "pursue an education," not just allow it to occur within them, as if this would be a possibility in any case. The students' role in the school community is to respond to the example of the teacher and become seekers of the truth in their own right. It is also important to note that Wojtyla speaks of this process of education as a responsibility which the students have in order to allow them to be prepared to move into the larger world community as its leaders.

The leaders and staff members of the school play a role in the development of the educational community as well. This role is played out, just as is the role of the teachers, through the example shown by them to the other members of the community. Wojtyla writes that the, "directors and administrators in a Catholic university promote the constant growth of the university and its community through a leadership of service; the dedication and witness of the non-academic staff are vital for the identity and life of the university" (Wojtyla/John Paul II, 1990a, No. 24). Here again it is possible to see the concept that a true community is based upon the giving of oneself to others and, ultimately, to the service of the truth, which is the school community's binding force.

By being a true *communio personarum* and formed as it is by those persons who are members of it, the school community does not and cannot replace the family as the primal educational community (Wojtyla, 1993, pp. 339–340). It does, however, need to possess the same qualities as the family community so as to effectively go about the work of educating the young person, and being, by definition, a true *communio personarum*. Wojtyla, returning to his more poetic writing style, presents this when he writes, concerning his own university experience,

> Alma mater. Alma mater Jagellonica...This is the name by which the university [the Jagiellonian University] is known, and it has profound significance. Mater— mother, namely, the one who gives birth, educates and trains. A university bears some resemblance to a mother. It is like a mother because of its maternal concern. This is a spiritual concern: that of giving birth to souls for the sake of knowledge, wisdom, the shaping of minds and hearts. (Wojtyla/John Paul II, 1997c, No. 4)

The school, in order to fulfill its role in the education of young persons, must establish and maintain a very real community which is modeled upon that found in the family.

In speaking of the university as being mother and acting with maternal concern for the members of its community, Wojtyla uses imagery which is reminiscent of some feminist educational literature, which emphasizes the need for caring in education. Nel Noddings (1992), as a representative of this literature, reminds her readers that, "women, more often than men, have been charged with the direct care of young children, the ill, and the aged," and while this may be taken to be a result of oppression, she indicates that "if we analyze the experience, we find considerable autonomy, love, choice...in the traditional female role" and that this experience can be evaluated as being "essential in developing fully human beings" (p. 24). It is unfortunate that Wojtyla has not developed this imagery further, as it would have been a point of departure for conversation with contemporary educational thought.

Wojtyla has noted that the binding force within every school community is the search for truth. For him, this search is more than just the fulfillment of the person's natural curiosity, but is, rather, a mode by which the human person can enter into the process of transcendence which leads, ultimately, to self-fulfillment. Wojtyla writes,

> The vocation of every university is to serve truth...Man transcends the boundaries of individual branches of knowledge in order to direct them towards that Truth and towards the definitive fulfillment of his own humanity. Here we can speak of the solidarity of the various branches of knowledge at the service of man, called to discover ever more completely the truth about himself and the world around him. (Wojtyla/John Paul II, 1997c, No. 4)

In his speaking of the importance of the search for truth to the development of the school community, it is possible once again to see the important role which truth plays in the self-fulfillment of the person, and, by extension, the education of the person. It is only by consciously relating one's human acts to the objective truth that one is able to transcend oneself, whether horizontally or vertically, and become more fulfilled.

Education in the Community of Humanity

The community of the family and the community of the school have been shown to be, for Wojtyla, indispensable elements in the education of the human person. In both of these communities, the individual person is provided with an atmosphere in which he can, by the gift of self and in reference to the truth, transcend his individuality and move towards self-fulfillment. Although it would seem that Wojtyla's philosophy of education would conclude here, his thought on education continues beyond the communities of family and school to the larger community of humanity. His ideas concerning education and the community of humanity are twofold: firstly, the larger community continuing the educative process and, secondly, the responsibility the educated person has toward the larger community of humanity. As was discussed above, the responsibility which the educated person has toward society at large should not be taken to mean that Wojtyla sees education as having a social end. Persons are not educated to bring about a good society, but rather bring about a good society because they are educated. Thus, a good society results from education but is not the end of education. In order to complete the process of understanding Wojtyla's view of education and the community, it is necessary to, at this time, take up these two points.

Wojtyla has unfolded the profound meaning of what it means to be in community as a human person. In order to understand what Wojtyla sees as the role of the community of humanity in education, it is necessary to recall the meaning of community for the person; specifically, that it is in community that the individual human person is able to experience transcendence and move toward self-fulfillment. Although Wojtyla specifically notes that education is carried out consciously in the communities of the family and school, each genuine *communio personarum* to which the individual belongs is, by his own definition of community, a place which furthers the end of education: the self-fulfillment of the human person.

It is in being open to this wider community of humanity, with its ever widening bands of diversity, that the human person is able to transcend self and progress toward the truth and self-fulfillment. Wojtyla hopes that, through the experience of education in the family and the school, that the young person will come to see the value of, and need for, being part of the larger community of humanity. He writes that at the very heart of Catholic education is community, which is not simply

> a concept to be taught, but as a reality to be lived...A sense of community implies openness to the wider community. Often today Catholic education takes place in changing neighborhoods; it requires a respect for cultural diversity, love for those of different ethnic backgrounds...without discrimination. Help your students to see themselves as members of the universal Church and the world community. (Wojtyla/John Paul II, 1987b, p. 155)

It is just such an appreciation for the wider community of humanity which will allow each person to continue the process of self-education culminating in self-fulfillment.

What Wojtyla envisions is a realization that each person within the human community should be open to learning by being in relation to other persons. As has been seen, being in the wider human community allows the person to continue the process of education begun in the family and school communities. Unfortunately, the reverse is also the case: the intentional removal of oneself from being in community with others, even in the family or school community, will seriously harm the process of education and self-fulfillment. More will be said regarding this below, when the issues of participation, alienation, and solidarity are discussed.

Having established the need for the human person to experience participation within the wider community of humanity, Wojtyla is very quick to point out the responsibility which accompanies being educated. It has been seen that throughout his entire philosophical anthropology, Wojtyla has always been concerned with "right" or moral behavior. In his philosophy of education he is no different: a person proceeds through the process of education by continually referencing one's acts to the objective truth, the objective norm. This understanding leads Wojtyla to a discussion of the responsibilities which the educated person has and also the duty which the school community has in fostering this sense of responsibility.

In speaking to university professors in his native Poland, Wojtyla reminded them that,

> There are few things as important in human life and society as the service of thought. Every intellectual, independently of his personal convictions, is called to let himself be guided by this sublime and difficult ideal and to function as a critical conscience regarding all that endangers humanity or diminishes it. Being a scholar entails obligations! (Wojtyla/John Paul II, 1997c, No. 5)

For Wojtyla, being educated means that one must be a person who works to make changes in society for the betterment of all people. This is so because, through the participation in the communities of the family and the school, the educated person has come to the realization that it is only by the gift of self to other persons that the individual can come to transcendence and fulfillment. With this in mind, Wojtyla is able to tell university faculty members that,

> University students, for example, are in a splendid position to take to heart the gospel invitation to go out of themselves, to reject introversion and to concentrate on the needs of others...What is at stake is not only the rectitude of individual human hearts, but also the whole social order as it touches the spheres of economics, politics and human rights and relations. (Wojtyla/John Paul II, 1987c, p. 163)

As Wojtyla's understanding of what should occur in the educated person is presented, it should be kept in mind that this going out of the self, this call to service of the greater community of humanity, is not the *reason for* education, but the *result of* education. Because education works toward providing the community in which the person can come to ever greater self-fulfillment, a person who has achieved a certain measure of self-fulfillment will naturally tend toward giving of self to another. In other words, education's result is a move away from individuality toward community, from selfishness to selflessness, from loneliness to love.

In his play, *The Radiation of Fatherhood*, Wojtyla reminds his readers that the human person can be said to be in God's image because God is a community of divine persons *and* chose to give of self by being Father. The human person is not self-fulfilled when in isolation; even though one desires to be self-sufficient, the ensuing loneliness is unbearable. The play has the first man, Adam, mulling over this odd situation in his mind. By being asked to accept fatherhood, Adam is called to move out of himself and yet he desires to retain his independence, even though it brings the pain of loneliness. Adam says,

> He [God] is lonely, I thought. What will make me more like Him, that is to say, independent of everything? Ah, to stand apart from everything, so that I could be only within myself! I should then be closest to You. I later said to Him, complaining, "You could have left me in the sphere of fertility (I would somehow have reconciled myself to nature) without placing me in the depths of a fatherhood to which I am unequal! Why did you plant it [fatherhood] in my soul? Was it not enough that you had it in yourself? (Wojtyla, 1987a, p. 336)

By the closing lines of the play, Adam, through the forming of a family community with the Woman, is able to grasp that human persons are most self-fulfilled when they give of themselves. Education, when properly experienced, produces the same result.

In addition to the educated student having a responsibility of service toward and for the community of humanity, the school community has the responsibility to do the same by the concrete example it offers to its students. The school community is also called upon to give of itself for the good of others. Wojtyla writes,

> The Christian spirit of service to others for the promotion of social justice is of particular importance for each Catholic university, to be shared by its teachers and developed in its students. The Church is firmly committed to the integral growth of all men and women. (Wojtyla/John Paul II, 1990a, No. 34)

It is very clear from reading Wojtyla's words that this service to the wider community is not an option for a school on whatever level; it is an integral part of fulfilling its educational mission: the self-fulfillment of the human person.

Although Wojtyla specifically notes service by the school community as being carried out by acts of social justice, he also emphasizes another aspect of the school community giving of itself. This aspect is in working towards developing the culture of humanity by its own research. While this aspect of service is more likely to be carried out on the post-secondary and graduate school levels, there are applications for all school communities. Wojtyla notes that,

> A Catholic university, as any university, is immersed in human society; as an extension of its service to the Church and always within its proper competence, it is called on to become an ever more effective instrument of cultural progress for individuals as well as for society. (Wojtyla/John Paul II, 1990a, No. 32)

In sum, the school community must not concern itself with only those problems and difficulties which directly effect it, but must see itself in solidarity with the community of humanity in facing problems of more universal proportions.

Participation and Educational Communities

It should be recalled that in Wojtyla's thought, simply being in the presence of other human persons does not mean that a true community of persons is formed. What is necessary for the establishment of a *communio personarum* is the ability of all persons, who are said to be in that community, to be involved with each other on the level of horizontal transcendence. Wojtyla (1993) states that participation should

> be seen as an authentic expression of personal transcendence and as a subjective confirmation of this transcendence in the person...That is why in *The Acting Person* it seemed possible to define participation (in its social profile) as a property by virtue of which human beings tend (also) toward self-fulfillment and fulfill themselves by acting and existing together with others. (p. 254)

From this definition it is very clear that the person must have participation in the community in order for self-fulfillment to come about. With this understanding of participation in mind, it is obvious that the ability for persons to participate in the communities of family and school is absolutely essential if the purpose of education is to be achieved. Thus the family and the school communities must be places where individual persons sense and know that they are fully participating members of these respective communities.

In recognizing the need for participation in the family and school communities in order for education to take place, it is necessary to attempt to come to an understanding of what it means, concretely, for a person to be able to participate in the community. Arriving at this understanding is not an easy task because Wojtyla himself does not lay out a clear blueprint of the process or what it specifically requires. He does, however, give to his readers enough of an idea, based upon his previous definitions of what the human person is and has the right to, from which construct a workable understanding of what it means to be able to participate in community. Concerning the mode in which participation is brought into being, Wojtyla (1993) writes that participation,

> is certainly not already a full blown reality merely as a result of my conceptualizing or becoming aware of the fact of another's humanity. In order for me to regard the other or a neighbor as another "I," I must become aware of and experience, among the overall properties of that other "human being," the same kind of property that determines my own "I," for this will determine my relationship to the other as an "I." (p. 202)

Participation, then, comes about when each person within the community is treated by every other member as a self-possessed person. This means that within the true *communio personarum*, each person has the freedom to perform human acts; has the freedom to make their own choices based upon the relation of a particular action to the truth. Simply phrased, participation exists when the full human personhood of each member of the community is honored.

When a person is able to participate in the community, there is created a reality significantly greater than a mere social organization. Each participating member of the community is able to come to very deep knowledge of the other members of the community. Thus the "I" is no longer in relation to just other human beings, but to other persons. Wojtyla (1993) notes that,

> Participation signifies a basic personalization of the relationship of one human being to another. I cannot experience another as I experience myself, because my own "I" as such is nontransferable. When I experience another person as a

person, I come as close as I can to what determines the other's "I" as the unique
and unrepeatable reality of that human being. (p.202)

This very real knowledge of the other person is what will cause each
member of the community to value all the others. In concrete terms, the
existence of participation on the level of the family and school
communities, and for that matter, in any community of persons, means
that no member of the community is used as an object to accomplish a
particular end. Participation means that each member of the community is
a subject and must have the ability and freedom to be part of what goes
on.

Unfortunately, as Wojtyla notes, even in social groups where there is
enough participation to say that the group is a *communio personarum*, it is
possible to have members who are alienated, members who are not able
to participate because of the current structure of the community. He
writes,

Alienation basically means the negation of participation, for it renders
participation difficult or even impossible. It devastates the "I-Other" relationship,
weakens the ability to experience another human being as another "I," and
inhibits the possibility of friendship and the spontaneous powers of community
(*communio personarum*). (Wojtyla, 1993, p. 206)

The person who is alienated cannot be a part of the "spontaneous powers"
of the community. From what we have seen, these "spontaneous powers"
are transcendence and self-fulfillment. In no uncertain terms, therefore, an
educational community, whether the family or the school, must have the
participation of all members in order to be able to bring about its original
purpose, the self-fulfillment of the students.

Although each member of the educational community must have
participation, Wojtyla does not envision the community being a perfect
democracy. He recognizes that there are legitimate roles to be played by
each member and that each member thereby has legitimate responsibilities
within that role (Wojtyla/John Paul II, 1994b, No. 15). This acceptance of
the various roles each member of the community has is discussed by
Wojtyla when he speaks of *solidarity*.

Solidarity and Educational Communities

For Wojtyla, solidarity has two basic components: the community's common good and a desire to work towards that common good. In regard to solidarity, he states that, "the attitude of solidarity is, so to speak, the natural consequence of the fact that human beings live and act together" (Wojtyla, 1979a, pp. 284-285). Additionally, as was presented above, the community's knowledge of and acceptance of its particular common good is what leads to participation by the members of the community because they are aware of what their freely chosen human acts are directed towards.

The common good is, in a sense, that reason for which the community exists, why it came together as a community of persons in the first place. Obviously, the reason why the community exists governs how each of the members are called upon to participate. In language more appropriate to education today, the term *common good* could well be substituted with the term *vision*. For the educational community to become a true *communio personarum*, all members must know and accept as valid why it exists; they must know what its common good or vision is. It is in knowing this common good and entering into the spirit of solidarity that each member chooses to freely act towards that good. Wojtyla notes that,

> In accepting the attitude of solidarity man does what he is supposed to do not only because of his membership in the group, but because he has the "benefit of the whole" in view: he does it for the "common good." The awareness of the common good makes him look beyond his own share; and this intentional reference allows him to realize essentially his own share. (Wojtyla, 1979a, p. 285)

When solidarity is present, participation is not called into question; members wish to participate and their contribution is recognized as intrinsic to the good of the whole.

Solidarity, for Wojtyla, also means an acceptance by each member of the community of their proper manner of participation. Each person recognizes his own unique contribution and this contribution is valued. He writes,

> Indeed, to some extent, solidarity prevents trespass upon other people's obligations and duties, and seizing things belonging to others...The attitude of solidarity means respect for all parts that are the share of every member of the community. To take over the duties and obligations that are not mine is

> intrinsically contrary to participation and to the essence of the community.
> (Wojtyla, 1979a, p. 285)

It is in the accepting of the common good, or vision, that the members of the community are able to actualize their participation in the community. In regard to the educational community, this enables each member to move toward the self-fulfillment which is the *raison d'être* of the family and school communities.

In concluding this discussion on solidarity, it is legitimate to ask questions regarding the applicability of this concept to any community of persons, educational or other. There is little doubt that applying it would require a great amount of work, especially for those members of the community who would be called upon to change the most. This being said, the value of true solidarity for the good of the person more than outweighs the work involved. Kevin Doran comes to much the same conclusion and his words will be left to conclude this discussion on solidarity. He writes, commenting on the practicality of solidarity, that

> Solidarity is practical because it is a dynamic principle of action, which enables a
> person to find support in community for his individual commitment to the
> common good, and to lend his support to a similar commitment on the part of
> other persons. In solidarity, the commitment of all the community members is
> greater than the sum of their individual commitments. (Doran, 1996, p. 241)

How Inclusive are Participation and Solidarity?

Throughout all of Wojtyla's philosophical writings, and, for that matter, his theological as well, he has made a continued appeal to the use of experience in arriving at certain philosophical truths. This has been done most notably when he has defended the existence of an objective, knowable, truth. Given this appeal to experience, it is important to ask: is the experience cited inclusive of the entire spectrum of human persons?

One aspect of this issue asks if Wojtyla can rely on experience leading to a universal norm for both men *and* women since he is a man himself and bound by the male biased Christian metanarrative? Lisa Sowle Cahill (1994) summarizes the issue by stating that feminists often call attention to

> women's actual experience in order to challenge "universals" which, they claim,
> reflect the biases of those in power. American and European women zestfully
> dismantle culture-bound gender stereotypes by celebrating the "differences" and

uniqueness of previously excluded voices. Feminists may rightly claim that many traditional Christian depictions of their natural or divinely mandated roles do not correspond to the reality and value of women's own lives. (p. 54)

Wojtyla would respond that the experience upon which he builds his philosophical anthropology is trans-gender in that it is common to both women and men. This is, he would argue, precisely what is meant by saying that the experience is universal—it would not be a universal experience if it were common to men only. Further, there is a danger of falling into the belief that there is nothing that can be said to be common experience between men and women. Cahill herself acknowledges this when she writes of "the danger of replacing oppressive generalizations with bottomless particularity...It is important to move back from particularity to a sense of shared human values which is so central to natural law" (1994, pp. 54-55). Wojtyla would hold that his use of experience would fall into the category of shared human values.

Another facet to this same question arises in regard to women's ability to be fully participating members of the community of the Church since they are unable to share their gift through the ordained ministry. Additionally, given Wojtyla's position as pope, isn't there a contradiction between his continued ban on the ordination of women and his philosophical understanding of community, participation, and solidarity? Wojtyla would respond by recalling his discussion of the importance of respecting the role each person has been given to perform in any particular community. He would also add that a difference in roles within the community in no way implies inequality; whether a person is the principal of the school or the attendance clerk, he or she is a contributing, necessary and equal member of the school community.

It is in discussing this issue, once again, that the difficulty in dealing with the two distinct roles which Wojtyla plays, as philosopher and as authoritative teacher, comes forward. There is no way to know in what manner Wojtyla the philosopher would have responded to the issue of women's mode of participation within the Church, but his philosophical circle of acquaintances was in no way gender restricted, nor were the groups of university students whom Wojtyla interacted with on a regular basis. It would be unfair, and, for that matter, contrary to the evidence, to suggest that Wojtyla views women as inferior or that he is sexist. Within the world of academia and education of the young, Wojtyla should be viewed as a person who accepted the inclusion of all.

For Wojtyla the authoritative teacher, women's roles within the Church seem to be more restricted, at least when it comes to the ordained ministry. How this exclusion can be reconciled with Wojtyla's previous philosophical thought is outside the intended scope of this study. A fuller discussion of the pertinent issues has been provided by Benedict Ashley (1996) in his text, *Justice in the Church: Gender and Participation,* which presents some of the possible philosophical responses which Wojtyla might offer to defend his position. This text, however, still must deal with the issue of Wojtyla's dual roles and therefore may not provide a clear understanding of Wojtyla's philosophical position.

VI

YOUTH AND EDUCATION

Throughout the preceding chapters, Karol Wojtyla's writings have been examined with the hope of drawing forth from them his philosophy of education. The writings thus far examined were clearly philosophical in nature, even when they moved into areas of theological discussion, and rightly so, since this study seeks to present Wojtyla's philosophy of education, not simply his theory of education. This chapter, however, will deal with writings which are decidedly not philosophical in nature. What is found herein is an examination of Wojtyla's writings directed to young people, where Wojtyla is seen as a pastor exhorting his flock rather than as a philosopher presenting his theory. These writings represent Wojtyla's desire to be an encouragement to the young people of the world: he is positive and upbeat, avoiding any of the negativity sometimes present when members of an older generation speak to members of a younger.

As has been noted numerous times in the preceding chapters, Wojtyla has spent a large portion of his pastoral energies with young people. Whether as a parish priest taking young people on retreats and outings or as a college professor teaching, conferring with or counseling his students, he brought with him to the papacy a wealth of experiences with young people (Malinski, 1979, p. 106 ff.). Additionally, much of his pre-papal writings were composed for the benefit of his younger parishioners and students, in order to help prepare them for making vocational choices (Wojtyla, 1981b, p. 9).

Coming to the papacy with this very youth-centered background makes Wojtyla unique among his papal predecessors. It is this background that has led to his large corpus of papal writings and allocutions composed specifically *for* young people, not just *about* young people. Of particular note within this corpus is his letter *To the Youth of the World* (Wojtyla/John Paul II, 1985) which was written on the occasion of the United Nations' International Youth Year in 1985. This rather substantial work presents Wojtyla's central themes and ideas regarding youth to which he will return in almost all of his subsequent letters and talks.

It was the celebration of the International Youth Year which led to a biennial gathering of young people from around the world with Wojtyla, each gathering taking place in a different host country. For each of these gatherings or pilgrimages, Wojtyla composed a "letter of invitation" which also highlighted the central theme of the gathering. Additionally, numerous talks and homilies were given by Wojtyla himself, during the pilgrimage, expounding upon the previously announced theme. The content of these letters of invitation, now numbering eight, as well as the talks and homilies given at the event, provide a wealth of information regarding Wojtyla's understanding of, and approach to, young people.

There can be little doubt as to Wojtyla's involvement with young persons, both before and after coming to the papacy, yet the question may legitimately be asked as to the significance of this involvement and these writings to youth toward understanding Wojtyla's philosophy of education. The significance for this study comes from the fact that it is in these writings and allocutions to youth that one finds the concrete application of much of the philosophical theorizing on education seen in Wojtyla's other works as analyzed in the preceding chapters. When dealing directly with young persons, whether in written or spoken word, Wojtyla seeks to help them understand who they are as persons as well as how they are called to self-fulfillment through self-education. By examining these various documents, it is hoped that a much less theoretical side of Wojtyla's educational philosophy will emerge; it is in these documents that the reader will begin to see how Wojtyla himself might direct his own students through the educative process. While a much more concrete application of his educational philosophy will emerge, it should be continually recalled that even these documents do not bring with them the personal interaction between student and educator, so central to Wojtyla's philosophical understanding of education.

What follows, then, is a presentation which will assist the reader in coming to understand exactly what the period of youth in a person's life is about and how the process of self-education needs to take place. This glimpse will provide, however, the needed discussion concerning the role of the student in order to assess what contribution Wojtyla has made toward a distinctively Catholic philosophy of education.

Before proceeding with an examination of Wojtyla's writings to young people, it should be noted that Wojtyla himself does not give a specific range of years for this period of youth. It is safe to say that he sees this period as encompassing from approximately age 11 through to the early 20s; thus, the junior high school, high school, and college years. This being said, it is important to realize that while Wojtyla's educational philosophy, thus far presented, is valid for the younger child and the adult learner as well. This chapter will concern itself only with examining what Wojtyla has to say to and about persons who are in the period of youth and their process of education.

The Qualities of Youth

The Value of the Period of Youth for the Person. Throughout all of his writings and allocutions to young people, Wojtyla continually emphasizes the goodness present in the qualities of youth. Before examining some of these qualities and how they relate to the educational process, it is important to note the very positive manner in which Wojtyla approaches young people. This positive manner comes from a very deep seated belief in the importance of the period of youth in the life of the human person. Youth is not a span of years that must be endured in order to arrive at adulthood, but is, rather, for Wojtyla, a time that must be savored and lived so as to have a fulfilled adulthood. He writes that the period of youth is a time of,

> intense discovery of the human "I" and of the properties and capacities connected with it. Before the inner gaze of the developing personality of the young man or woman, there is gradually and successively revealed that specific and in a sense unique and unrepeatable potentiality of a concrete humanity, in which there is as it were inscribed the whole plan of future life. Life presents itself as the carrying-out of that plan: as self-fulfillment. (Wojtyla/John Paul II, 1985, No. 3)

It is because Wojtyla understands the importance of the period of youth in the life of the human person that he has devoted so much of his time to young people in order to help them appreciate this importance (Wojtyla/John Paul II, 1994c, p. 123).

The importance of this period in the life of the person thus acknowledged, it must also be noted that Wojtyla sees in the period of youth a great responsibility placed on each young person as well. This responsibility is to continue the search for life's ultimate meaning, to continue to ask questions which will allow this search to continue and ultimately to decide on one's vocation in life. To use Wojtyla's philosophical terminology, which he very much avoids in his exchanges with young people, the responsibility during this period is to continue the process of self-education, leading ever more towards self-fulfillment.

The understanding of this fundamental importance of the period of youth, and of its concomitant responsibilities on young people, is of utmost importance for all those working with young people—whether parents, teachers or pastors. Wojtyla points out that he himself came to this realization early in his ministry. He writes, speaking of his own insights derived from his pastoral involvement with young people, that youth is a time,

> given by Providence to every person and given to him as a responsibility. During that time he searches, like the young man in the gospel [Matthew 19: 16–22], for answers to basic questions; he searches not only for the meaning of life but also for a concrete way to go about living his life. Every mentor...must be aware of this characteristic and must know how to identify it in every boy and girl. I will say more: He *must love this fundamental aspect of youth.* (Wojtyla/John Paul II, 1994c, pp. 120–121)

This quote provides an understanding not only of the period of youth, but also the importance, for Wojtyla, of having adults in the young person's world who not only understand the import of this time of life but who also want to be involved in assisting the young person through this period.

Approaching young people by emphasizing the immense importance of this period of their lives has enabled Wojtyla to continue to attract many young people to the World Youth Day celebrations. Many of the young people interviewed at the conclusion of the World Youth Day pilgrimage which took place in Denver, Colorado, in August of 1993 spoke of "feeling important" after listening to Wojtyla. "His words gave the young people an immediate sense of mission. 'Teenagers get tired of hearing they are the future of the Church,' said Sherman, who said the pope's message was that they could be active members of the Church now, not years down the road. 'I walked away realizing my part in the Church and my responsibility to the Church,' said Maureen Kelly" (Lorsung, 1993, p. 31). Although many have questioned whether young people actually listen to and follow Wojtyla's words, especially those dealing with sexual morality, there seems to be little doubt that young people have not missed Wojtyla's emphasis on the importance of this period in their lives.

In addition to bringing to young people this emphasis on the importance of this period of their lives, Wojtyla also maintains an extremely optimistic view regarding the young people of society; a view which is often not shared by many adults. He writes, "In the young there is, in fact, an immense potential for good and for creative possibility" (Wojtyla/John Paul II, 1994c, p. 124). It is this positive sense of the innate goodness of the young people of the world that has continued to bring young people to hear Wojtyla, even as he advances in years. He has publicly acknowledged the feelings of many people that gatherings of young people, for the World Youth Day events, would be problematic yet Wojtyla continued to express his belief in the goodness of the young. While visiting New York in 1995, he stated,

> I remember clearly that many people wondered and worried that the young people of America would not come to the World Youth Day, or, if they did come, that they would be a problem. Instead, the young people's joy, their hunger for the truth, their desire to be united all together in the Body of Christ, made clear to everyone that many, very many young people of America have values and ideals which seldom make the headlines. (Wojtyla/John Paul II, 1995a, No. 1)

This optimistic view of young people naturally leads to the question of precisely what qualities do young people have which have caused Wojtyla to maintain his positive outlook. It is a presentation of some of these qualities which will now be addressed.

The Inquisitive Nature of Youth. One need not do more than enter a room full of small children to realize that childhood is a time of great inquisitiveness. Wojtyla clearly recognizes this; however, his presentation regarding the inquisitive nature of the young person goes far beyond the simple "why" questions found among little children. Young people do ask their own particular set of "why" questions, according to Wojtyla, but these questions are of a much more metaphysical nature; in the period of youth, answers are sought to some of life's more difficult questions. He writes,

> What must I do? What must I do to inherit eternal life? What must I do so that my life may have full value and full meaning? The youth of each one of you, dear friends, is a treasure that is manifested precisely in these questions. Man asks himself these questions throughout his life. But in the time of youth they are particularly urgent, indeed insistent. And it is good that this is so. (Wojtyla/John Paul II, 1985, No. 3)

Thus the inquisitiveness of youth is most clearly found in the first attempts to answer questions which have puzzled and perplexed the human race since the beginning. In addition to the questions already mentioned by Wojtyla in the above quote, the following may be added: Why do I exist? What is my purpose? Is there a God? (Lorsung, 1993, p. 120).

All of these questions, Wojtyla maintains, are very natural but at the same time they can be the cause of much anxiety, especially when young people do not have the guidance and support of adults. In addition to being the cause of anxiety, these questions, if answered badly, can be the cause of much pain and suffering in youth and on into adulthood. Wojtyla notes that this is the case for many young people in the world. In his *Letter to Youth*, he writes,

> These essential questions are asked in a special way by those members of your generation whose lives have been weighed down since childhood by suffering: by some physical lack or defect, some handicap or limitation, or by a difficult family or social situation...How many are forced from childhood to live in an institution or hospital, condemned to a certain passivity which can make them begin to feel that they are of no use to humanity! (Wojtyla/John Paul II, 1985, No. 3)

Here it is possible to detect Wojtyla's concern that all young people have the opportunity to participate in the communities in which they find themselves. It is when they feel isolated and removed (or alienated, to use Wojtyla's terminology) from their community that the process of self-education breaks down, resulting in the feelings mentioned in the above text.

Thus, while inquisitiveness is good and an integral part of the process of self-education, it is easily sidetracked by circumstances; circumstances not necessarily of the young person's own making. When circumstances do sidetrack the efforts of the young person to come to terms with these life questions, fear, uncertainty, isolation, and loneliness often result, bringing with them a host of other plagues against young people. Asking young people to recall their possible fear of the dark when they were younger, Wojtyla writes that there are still certain "darknesses" which can haunt youth today. He writes that there is,

> another kind of darkness in the world: the darkness of doubt and uncertainty. You may feel the darkness of loneliness and isolation. Your anxieties may come from questions about your future, or regrets about past choices. Sometimes the world itself seems filled with darkness...There is something terribly wrong when

so many young people are overcome by hopelessness to the point of taking their own lives. (Wojtyla/John Paul II, 1999, No. 2)

It is for this reason that the period of youth in the life of a person must be taken seriously and recognized as integral to the self-fulfillment of the human person—which is the goal of education for Wojtyla.

The Excitement for Life in the Young Person. Despite the fact that young people do experience the difficulties mentioned above, Wojtyla also sees that there is an excitement and vitality for life which exists in the hearts of the young. Here again Wojtyla makes a definite effort to remind the adults to whom he speaks to respect this vitality and enthusiasm and recognize in it the goodness of God. He writes,

> We need the enthusiasm of the young. We need their *joie de vivre*. In it is reflected something of the original joy God had in creating man. The young experience the same joy within themselves. This joy is the same everywhere, but it is also ever new and original. The young know how to express this joy in their own special way. (Wojtyla/John Paul II, 1994c, p. 125)

This enthusiasm, in Wojtyla's understanding, stems from the process of self-education; as young persons begin to come to terms with life's more complex questions, they feel within themselves the continual creation of themselves as persons. They are enthusiastic about life because, as Wojtyla mentions in the preceding quote, they sense the joy of creating themselves—this joy being similar to the divine joy at the creation of the world. This being said, there is also the danger that this enthusiasm can be dampened or even smothered by events and circumstances in which young people find themselves today. Wojtyla is adamant that adults must respond to this enthusiasm and encourage it, as well as trying to rectify any situations which could destroy this youthful excitement for life.

When speaking about the effect which youthful excitement can have on adults, Wojtyla returns to his own personal experience. He has, time and time again, made reference to the fact that he is "energized" by his meetings with young people and those who travel with him have noted the same thing. Wojtyla writes, "Even though he [Wojtyla himself] is getting older, they [young people] urge him to be young, they do not permit him to forget his experience, his discovery of youth and its great importance for the life of every man" (Wojtyla/John Paul II, 1994c, p. 125). In a more subtle and extemporaneous manner, when presented with a hockey stick and jersey by a group of young Americans, he expressed the same idea when he said: "So, I am prepared to return once more to play hockey! But if I will be able to, that is the question. Perhaps after this meeting I will be a bit more ready!" (Wojtyla/John Paul II, 1999, No. 6).

From what he has written or spoken, both to young people and to adults, Wojtyla firmly believes that adults have the responsibility to respond to the enthusiasm of the young and to allow this response to reawaken their own experience of youth. This reawakening has merit because it will hopefully move the adult person to revisit the questions regarding life which they first sought to answer in their own years of youth.

Love and the Gift of Self. Another quality which Wojtyla speaks of at length in almost all his communications with young people is love, and its corollary, the gift of self. Both of these ideas are integral to his personalistic philosophy and his basic understanding of life vocation, but they find an important place in his writings to young people because it is in youth that they are first awakened. Love for others finds its basis for Wojtyla in humanity's basic communal nature; love arises when the human person realizes that "it is not good that the man should be alone" (Genesis 2:18, Revised Standard Version). It is in coming to an understanding of this communal nature, as was discussed at length above, that allows human persons to define themselves *qua* persons. Wojtyla writes,

> If at every stage of his life man desires to be his own person, to find love, during his youth he desires it even more strongly...Clearly, then, the fundamental problem of youth is profoundly personal. In life, youth is when we come to know ourselves. It is also a time of communion. Young people, whether boys or girls, know they must live for and with others, they know that their life has meaning to the extent that it becomes a free gift for others. (Wojtyla/John Paul II, 1994c, p. 121)

As can be discerned from this quote, Wojtyla believes that young people naturally have this sense of the need to give of oneself to others. Whether this natural sense is built upon is another question, but it is something Wojtyla sees as part of the nature of being young. Building upon this sense is part of self-education, accomplished with the guidance of parents, teachers, and mentors.

Because of the importance of giving of self in order to enter into the process of horizontal and vertical transcendence, and thus self-fulfillment, Wojtyla devotes much of his energy to reminding young people of this important dimension of their youth. He writes,

> Each one of us belongs to a great family, in which he has his own place and his own role to play. Selfishness makes people deaf and dumb; love opens eyes and hearts, enabling people to make that original and irreplaceable contribution which, together with the thousands of deeds of so many brothers and sisters, often distant and unknown, converges to form the mosaic of charity which can change the tide of history. (Wojtyla/John Paul II, 1995b, No. 6)

What is clear from this quote, in addition to the importance of giving of self, is the dignity of each individual human person. Wojtyla reminds young people of their uniqueness and the donation which only their unique selves may bring to the world. He also reminds them that there is a needed reciprocity: one must be willing to receive the gift of others as well as give of themselves. It is this reciprocity which brings horizontal transcendence into existence.

In many of Wojtyla's writings concerning young people, some of which have been examined thus far, there has been an often harsh critique of the current world culture. One might be tempted to believe that Wojtyla would advocate that young people remove themselves from the current scene in order to remain "uncontaminated," so to speak. This however would be an incorrect assumption. On the contrary, Wojtyla makes it clear that young persons must be part of the culture in which they find themselves. He writes,

> It is our duty then to live in history, side by side with our peers, sharing their worries and hopes, because the Christian is and must be fully a man of his time. He cannot escape into another dimension, ignoring the tragedies of his era, closing his eyes and heart to the anguish that pervades life. On the contrary, it is he who, although not "of" this world, is immersed "in" this world every day, ready to hasten to wherever there is a brother in need of help, a tear to be dried, a request for help to be answered. (Wojtyla/John Paul II, 1995b, No. 4)

It is by this involvement and, thereby, giving of oneself, that the young person may bring about the needed changes in any given societal culture.

While any culture clearly influences those living in it, Wojtyla would recoil against any suggestion that the human person is permanently enslaved to any given culture and powerless to bring about a cultural "revolution."

Having examined some of the qualities of youth, as understood by Wojtyla, it is now possible to turn to the process whereby a young person moves along the road to self-fulfillment, the goal of Wojtyla's understanding of education.

The Young Person and Truth

As has been seen above in the examination of Wojtyla's philosophy of the person, truth plays an integral role in the proper road toward self-fulfillment. Because truth is the touchstone of the human intellect, education can only come about when truth is sought after. It should come as no surprise, therefore, that Wojtyla will continually speak to young people about the importance of seeking the truth in order for them to enter into the processes of both self-education and self-fulfillment. He writes,

> However, when we discuss the question of education, study, learning and school, there emerges a question of fundamental importance for the human person, and in a special way for a young person. This is the question of truth. Truth is the light of the human intellect...The knowledge which frees man does not depend on education alone...though education, the systematic knowledge of reality, should serve the dignity of the human person. It should therefore serve the truth. (Wojtyla/John Paul II, 1985, No. 12)

It is in this continual pursuit of the truth that the young person will be able to transcend self and thereby move toward self fulfillment, which is the goal of education.

Truth is, when all is said and done, the eternal reference point for the human person. It is only when a young person makes use of this reference point that a life worthy of a human person can be lived. While it is seemingly obvious that education seeks to impart truth in regard to the subject matter being taught, Wojtyla's emphasis on the role of truth in the life of the young person aims at a much more significant target. The target which Wojtyla tries to put into the sight of the young people he speaks to is the truth about the human person; the dignity which the person possesses as well as the teleology of the person. He writes,

I likewise hope that this "growth" [in stature and wisdom] will come about
through contact with the achievements of humanity, and still more through
contact with living people...Youth seems particularly sensitive to the truth,
goodness and beauty contained in the works of humanity. Through contact with
people on the level of so many different cultures, of so many arts and sciences,
we learn the truth about man, the truth which can build up and enrich the
humanity of each one of us. (Wojtyla/John Paul II, 1985, No. 14)

Stated much more directly, Wojtyla is trying to explain to young people
that their experience or study of the world will help them on their way to
finding the truth about themselves as persons and to understand this truth.
When young people come to begin to understand this truth about
themselves, then they will be on the road to becoming self-educated.

It is important to note at this juncture that the search for the truth and
the process of becoming self-educated and self-fulfilled is not something
which Wojtyla would see as coming to an end. Although certain periods of
one's life may be more suited to this process, one is never able to say that
one has discovered all truth and therefore is in "possession" of all the
answers. As was discussed above, when speaking of the criticisms of
Wojtyla's metaphysical presuppositions, being in search of the truth does
not mean that any individual human person may possess the truth in its
purely objective form. Because each person brings his or her own personal
life experiences to any cognitive activity, the objective truth is always seen
through the eyes of each subject, thus explaining the differences of opinion
which arise between human persons. Persons will see reality in different
ways based upon their experiences and perception of those experiences.
Wojtyla's ultimate concern when speaking to young people is that this
subjective understanding of objective truth can lead to the assumption that
there is nothing that can be said to be objective (whether truth or in the
moral order). He continually cautions young people to avoid falling into
the trap of a purely subjective, and therefore relativistic, understanding of
the world, truth, the destiny of the human person, and the moral order.
Wojtyla sees that this can lead to seeking a basis for life which is not based
upon the truth but which is, rather, based upon what one wants to *believe*
the truth to be. He writes, speaking of false prophets who propose false
understandings of the human person, that some of these prophets,

condemn creation, and...lead thousands of young people along the paths of an
impossible liberation which eventually leaves them even more isolated...
Seemingly at the opposite extreme, there are the teachers of the "fleeting

moment," who invite people to give free rein to every instinctive urge or longing, with the result that individuals fall prey to a sense of anguish and anxiety leading them to seek refuge in false, artificial paradises, such as that of drugs. (Wojtyla/John Paul II, 1992, No. 3)

While Wojtyla makes clear to young people that the search for truth is the catalyst behind transcendence, self-education, and self-fulfillment, he also speaks to youth regarding the role of freedom in the search for truth. Given freedom's importance in Wojtyla's philosophical anthropology, an examination of how he explains human freedom to young people will now be taken up.

The Young Person and Freedom

It should be recalled that in Wojtyla's philosophical anthropology, the act of a human person is what allows that person to be known by others and it can only be said that the act of the person is revelatory in so far as the act was actually a human act, i.e., an act done in and with freedom. Additionally, this freedom to act is also intimately connected with the truth: if acts are freely chosen to be done in conformity with the truth, they are good and help the person move toward self-fulfillment; if the acts are not in conformity with the truth, they are evil and hinder the person from moving toward self-fulfillment. Given the relation between the truth and freedom, it should come as no surprise that Wojtyla takes up the concept of freedom, and its relation to truth, on a regular basis when he is interacting with young people.

Although Wojtyla refrains from presenting his philosophical understanding of the relationship between the truth and freedom in his addresses to young people, he does make the connection between them abundantly clear. Urging them to reject the various popular slogans regarding freedom, Wojtyla explains to the young people of the United States that,

True freedom is a wonderful gift from God, and it has been a cherished part of your country's history. But when freedom is separated from truth, individuals lose their moral direction and the very fabric of society begins to unravel. Freedom is not the ability to do anything we want, whenever we want. Rather, freedom is the ability to live responsibly the truth of our relationship with God and with one another. (Wojtyla/John Paul II, 1999, No. 3)

Freedom, then, must always be understood within the context of searching for the truth. When freedom becomes separated from the truth in the quest for self-fulfillment, human persons are no longer in control of their own destiny and allow other persons or things to enslave them. He warns young people that,

> The human person, created in the image and likeness of God, cannot become a slave to things, to economic systems, to technological civilization, to consumerism, to easy success. Man cannot become the slave of his inclinations and passions, sometimes deliberately aroused. We must defend ourselves against this danger. (Wojtyla/John Paul II, 1997d, No. 4)

While Wojtyla reminds young people of the proper use of freedom, he also seeks to remind them of the price at which the personal freedom of self-education and self-fulfillment is often purchased. Totalitarian regimes have, most particularly in the 20th century, often denied the individual person the freedom to pursue self-education in order to bring self-fulfillment. Although Wojtyla has spoken of the need for young people to be free from the "slaveries" mentioned in the preceding quote, he has also spoken of the importance of governments and cultures to provide intellectual and personal freedom for its people. While on a visit to his Polish homeland, after the fall of the communist regime, Wojtyla reminded Polish youth of the sacrifices made in defense of truth and freedom. Speaking, in Poznan, about the death of workers protesting political and social oppression, Wojtyla stated that

> It would be difficult not to mention here...the Monument to the Victims of June 1956. I wanted to come to this Monument in 1983 when I made my first visit to your city as Pope, but on that occasion I was denied permission to pray beneath the Crosses of Poznan. I am pleased that today, together with you—the young Poland—I am able to pay homage to the workers who gave their lives in defense of truth, justice and the independence of our homeland. (Wojtyla/John Paul II, 1997d, No. 3)

In reminding the young people of Poland of the sacrifices made by others in defense of truth and the freedom to pursue the truth, Wojtyla is placing the challenge before all young people to continually be seekers of truth in the process of their own self-education, regardless of the possible personal cost.

The considerable emphasis placed upon freedom, and its role in seeking truth, by Wojtyla, is aimed at helping young people understand their own individual role in the process of self-education. Although self-education, as a concept and step toward self-fulfillment, has been examined at length above, it is important to revisit this concept by seeing how Wojtyla himself explains it to young people. This is the task which will be undertaken next.

Self-Education: The Role of the Young Person in Education

Throughout the preceding pages of this chapter, it has been possible to see how Wojtyla views the period of youth in the life of the human person and the importance of seeking the truth and freely choosing to act in accord with truth. This seeking for and freely acting in accord with truth is an ongoing process which constitutes the process of self-education, which Wojtyla understands to be the *sine qua non* of self-fulfillment, the ultimate purpose, or philosophical end, of the educative process. He writes,

> All this [seeking truth and freely acting in accord with it] constitutes the very kernel of what we call education, and especially what we call self education. Yes: self-education! For an interior structure of this kind, where "the truth makes us free,"—cannot be built only "from outside." Each individual must build this structure "from within"—build it with effort, perseverance and patience (which is not always so easy for young people). And it is precisely this structure which is called self-education. (Wojtyla/John Paul II, 1985, No. 13)

Not surprisingly, when one examines what Wojtyla has written or spoken to young people regarding self-education, what emerges is a relatively clear understanding of the role of the student in the entire enterprise of education.

From examining these various texts regarding self-education, one is struck by the incredibly active role which Wojtyla understands students to have in the process of their education. Students are not educated by being passive participants; sponges, so to speak, absorbing the water of knowledge pouring forth from parents and teachers. This active role is very consistent with the value he places on the period of youth in a person's life as well as the high estimation he has of the qualities of young people.

Wojtyla presents this active role to young people in no uncertain terms. He writes,

> For while there is no doubt that the family educates and that the school teaches and educates, at the same time both the action of the family and that of the school will remain incomplete (and could even be made useless) unless each one of you young people undertakes the work of your own education. Education in the family and at school can only provide you with a certain number of elements for the work of self-education. (Wojtyla/John Paul II, 1985, No. 13)

Although Wojtyla is very explicit and emphatic in presenting the importance of self-education to young people, he does not, unfortunately, translate this into concrete examples for the school.

This being said, however, it is not impossible to interpolate his statements into more practical terms. It appears that the family and school are called upon to continually present to the young person the multifarious discoveries of human culture. From these presentations, young persons must, using their own reason and conscience, decide for themselves to make these truths their own, and then act in accord with this knowledge. All the truths of humanity could be laid before young persons, but if they choose not to "make it their own," there is no education. With this understanding of self-education, it is obvious why Wojtyla was so strong a voice in support of the Second Vatican Council's *Decree on Religious Liberty* and other conciliar contributions calling for the respect of each person's conscience (Schmitz, 1993, pp. 110–111, 161). It is within this context that it is possible to again see Wojtyla's viewpoint regarding the truth: while there is an objective truth which can be known by the human person, this truth is always mediated through the individual, and therefore subjective, human person. This viewpoint must be kept in mind by parents and educators; the truth cannot be forced upon the young person, the young person must be guided and supported so as to come to the truth for themselves.

The importance of self-education for youth is of great importance, since it is as a young person that one's life direction or vocation is concretized. Wojtyla returns again and again to remind young people that the period of youth is not just a time to make plans to be carried out in the future. Youth is, he says, the period when personal development takes place which will allow for future plans to be carried out. Wojtyla writes that the future must begin to be accomplished in the period of youth since, through work, education, and especially through self-education, we create life itself, building the foundation of the successive development of our personality. In this sense, we can say that youth is "the sculptress that shapes the whole of life," and the form that youth gives to the concrete humanity of each of you is consolidated in the whole of life. (Wojtyla/John Paul II, 1985, No. 13)

The knowledge that youth is not just a period of waiting for "coming of age" underscores its importance as well as the societal imperative to make education possible for all. Introducing the young person into the process of self-education is, ultimately, that which will help to ensure a self-fulfilled person. While this is the goal of education, Wojtyla notes that the well-being of human culture and society rest upon individual human persons who are self-fulfilled. Thus, education for each person is also of benefit to society. He writes,

This fact [young people deprived of educational opportunity] is a permanent challenge to all those responsible for education on a national and international scale, that this state of affairs be appropriately improved. For education is one of the fundamental benefits of human civilization. It is especially important for the young. Upon it also depends to a great extent the future of the whole of society. (Wojtyla/John Paul II, 1985, No. 12)

Society, therefore, needs to provide education for all, not only because the dignity of the human person demands it, but also because society's survival depends upon it.

With Wojtyla emphasizing the duty governments and society have to provide for young people the opportunity for education, it must be noted that he also places the burden of becoming educated squarely on the shoulders of young people themselves. Education is work and must be responded to accordingly, by bringing to it diligence and effort. Again emphasizing that it is the role of students to be active in their own education, Wojtyla calls upon young people not to turn away from the work this entails, since work itself is part of the process of self-education. He states that,

Work—all work—is linked to effort...and this experience of hard work is shared by each one of you from your earliest years. At the same time, however, work in a specific way forms man, and in a certain sense creates him. So it is always a question of work which is creative...The work which characterizes the period of youth is...linked to the school. (Wojtyla/John Paul II, 1985, No. 12)

In recognizing that work itself is part of the process of self-education, Wojtyla helps to reinforce his belief that self-education does not end. It is a continual process which is life-long.

While much of Wojtyla's discussion of self-education involves the period of youth in a person's life, he does not see, as is noted above, self-education as something which ends when a person moves into adulthood. The controlling factor in continuing self-education is to be aware that the process needs to continue and that the experiences encountered throughout one's life are educative. The importance of self-education for youth, however, cannot be overlooked, since it is as a young person that one's life direction or vocation is concretized. While youth is a special time of self-education, all persons continue to be students, to be in the role of a student through work. Wojtyla writes,

> At school you have to acquire the intellectual, technical and practical skills that will enable you to take your place usefully in the great world of human work. But while it is true that the school has to prepare you for work, including manual work, it is equally true that work itself is a school in which great and important values are learned: it has an eloquence of its own which makes a valid contribution to human culture. (Wojtyla/John Paul II, 1985, No. 12)

This emphasis on the role which work plays in the development of the human person is an important theme for Wojtyla, one which he discussed in greater detail in his encyclical *Laborem Excercens* (Wojtyla/John Paul II, 1981c). Wojtyla's emphasis on work as continuing the process of self-education also leads directly to another dimension of the role of the student: to be fully interactive with human culture and society.

Because the human person is, by nature, communal, Wojtyla reminds young people of their role in helping to form human culture and society as well as how they can be formed by the culture and society in which they live. This "reciprocity of influence" recalls Wojtyla's concept of horizontal transcendence, one of the indispensable aspects of self-education and self-fulfillment. Thus, the culture and society in which a person lives contributes to the person's self-education; at the same time, through the process of self-education, the person is called upon to return to their culture the learning they have acquired. Wojtyla writes,

> The moral personality formed in this way [through self-education during youth] constitutes the most important contribution that you can make to life in the community, to the family, to society, to professional activity and also to cultural

and political activity...Each one of you must in some way contribute to the
richness of these communities, first of all by means of what he or she is.
(Wojtyla/John Paul II, 1985, No. 7)

This call to social activity by the student is another manner in which
Wojtyla continues to drive home the point that the student's role in
education is in no way a passive one. He writes, "Within nations we can
feel the strength of longing for unity that will break down every barrier of
indifference and hate. It is especially for you, young people, to take on the
great task of building a society where there will be more justice and
solidarity" (Wojtyla/John Paul II, 1990b, No. 4).

As was mentioned in the preceding paragraph, while Wojtyla
understands that one role of the student is to bring about transformation
of society and culture, he is equally cognizant of the role society and
culture have on the self-education of the young person. He writes, to
young people, that,

From its very beginning the history of humanity passes—and will do so until the
end—through the family. A man enters the family through the birth which he
owes to his parents, his father and mother, and at the right moment he leaves this
first environment of life and love in order to pass to a new one...If the family is
the first teacher of each one of you, at the same time—through the family—you
are also taught by the tribe, people or nation with which you are linked through
the unity of culture, language and history. (Wojtyla/John Paul II, 1985, No. 11)

From this quote it is clear that Wojtyla fully understands the role, for good
or evil, which culture and society play in a young person's self-education.

It is this understanding which has led to his often scathing critique of
20th century culture and society; it is also why he calls upon young people
to be instruments of change to bring about a culture and society based
upon the truth about the human person. In all of Wojtyla's writing to and
for young people, he has called them to look to Jesus Christ as the way to
discovering the truth about themselves (Wojtyla/John Paul II, 1991, No.
4). In order to apprehend the complete picture of Wojtyla's
"conversation" with young people, his words regarding the place of Jesus
Christ must be examined. It is this task which will now be taken up.

Jesus Christ as the Model for Youth

Given the pervasive nature of Jesus Christ in all of Wojtyla's letters, messages and homilies to young people, one could legitimately ask why this examination did not begin this chapter as opposed to bringing it to a conclusion. The placement of Wojtyla's words to youth regarding Jesus here was due to the desire to first understand what the period of life called "youth" was about, as well as to present Wojtyla's philosophical understanding before his theological. In this way, one may approach Wojtyla from a variety of angles, not just from his Christian perspective.

This being said, Wojtyla is clearly of the mind that Jesus offers to humanity the quintessential example of what it means to be fully self-educated and self-fulfilled. It is important to realize that, for Wojtyla, even those who do not believe in Jesus are able to embark upon the road to self-education and self-fulfillment. It would be doing Wojtyla a grave injustice to imply anything to the contrary. Wojtyla's message to young people concerning Jesus is that if they are looking for an example to follow in how to live their lives, they need look no further than Jesus and the message Jesus preached. Additionally, he calls upon young people to present Jesus as a model to others. He writes,

> Do not be afraid of presenting Christ to someone who does not yet know him. Christ is the true answer, the most complete answer to all the questions which concern the human person and his destiny. Without Christ the human person remains an insolvable riddle. Therefore, have the courage to present Christ! Certainly you must do this in a way which respects each person's freedom of conscience, but you must do it. (Wojtyla/John Paul II, 1991, No. 4)

It is important to note that in Wojtyla's presentation of Jesus as a model for self-education, he consistently reminds young people that following Jesus is not a question of following a set of rules or philosophical concepts. Rather, following Jesus means entering into a relationship with a real person, Jesus himself. He writes, concerning the young person's encounter with Jesus, that,

> It is Jesus who takes the initiative...He, indeed, has always loved us first (cf. 1 John 4:10). This is the fundamental dimension of the encounter: we are not dealing with something, but with Someone, with the "Living One." Christians are not the disciples of a system of philosophy: they are men and women who, in faith, have experienced the encounter with Christ. (Wojtyla/John Paul II, 1996, No. 2)

Moving even further in his presentation of the importance of this personal encounter with Jesus, Wojtyla speaks of the friendship that Jesus seeks with all his followers, a friendship which will show the young person what it means to be a friend to another person. Calling to mind that Jesus offers his friendship to each person, a friendship which is genuine, loyal, and total, Wojtyla calls young people to live out their friendships in the same way. He writes,

> This is how young people ought to relate to one another, for youth without friendship is impoverished and diminished. Friendship is nourished by sacrifice for the sake of serving one's friends and truly loving them. And without such sacrifice there can be no real friendship, no truly healthy youth, no future for one's country, no genuine religion. (Wojtyla/John Paul II, 1998b, No. 1)

All of Wojtyla's references to Jesus are meant to call young people into a relationship with Jesus Christ in order to help them in their own journey of self-education. He wants, aside from bringing more people to faith in Jesus, to help young people to see that if they live their lives after the example of Jesus, they will achieve the goal of education: self-fulfillment. He explains,

> Education in the Christian life is not limited to encouraging the individual's spiritual growth, even if initiation into a solid, regular life of prayer remains the principle and foundation of the building. Familiarity with the Lord, when it is genuine, necessarily leads us to think, choose and act as Christ thought, chose and acted." (Wojtyla/John Paul II, 1997e, No. 8)

Wojtyla is confident that, when self-education is entered into in a genuine search for the truth, young people will be receptive to entering into a relationship with the person of Jesus Christ. This relationship, however, can never be forced upon anyone, much less a young person, since this would be completely at odds with the person's dignity and work of self-fulfillment.

Having reviewed the major themes of Wojtyla's message to young people, it has been shown that Wojtyla has a deep and fundamental respect for young people. This respect is founded upon the importance of this period of a person's life in the process of self-education. Here, also, has been seen a much more concrete expression of Wojtyla's educational philosophy; how he would go about guiding young people through self-education and on toward self-fulfillment.

VII

THE MODEL CATHOLIC SCHOOL

As has been alluded to numerous times, Wojtyla has left a corpus of writings and allocutions which is extremely theoretical and, which, while important, needs to be moved into a more practical mode. This concluding chapter will attempt to do just that; take Wojtyla's theory and move it into practical application by verbally constructing the "model" Catholic school as envisioned by the theory presented. While not pretending to cover all the elements which go into the operation of a successful school, this presentation will cover the more pertinent ones, which will reflect Wojtyla's thought. Those currently engaged in the work of education might also use this chapter as a tool for assessing their own practices if they found Wojtyla's philosophy of education to be of value.

Karol Wojtyla Builds His Dream School

The Students. There is little doubt that, given Wojtyla's emphasis on the active nature of the students role, based upon his concept of self-education, that he would begin any discussion regarding his "dream school" with the students. The hallmark of the school would have to be that it is a community in which the personhood of every student is absolutely respected. This respect would therefore have to be taken into account regarding academics, extra-curricular activities, and discipline. The respect for the student's conscience in all areas of study, including religion, would also be safeguarded, since, as Wojtyla mentioned numerous times, only this is worthy of the dignity of the human person who acts in freedom. It would be through this emphasis on respecting the personhood of each student that the students would be able to come to an understanding of what it means to be a person-in-community. In other words, how to begin the process of horizontal transcendence so necessary for true self-education to begin and flourish.

Wojtyla's school would have no place for any *institutional* degradation of the students' personhood and would need to be continually examining itself in order to work towards eliminating any policy which treated students as objects instead of persons. This objectification of the student could take many forms, such as viewing students as a means of making the school "look good" or having students in the school simply to keep enrollment at an economically sound level, even if the educational program offered does not meet their needs. At any rate, Wojtyla's school would work to be a place where all decisions were based upon what was best for the personal development of each student. In seeking to put forward this objective, the school's common good would also be furthered.

In a school which fully respected the personhood of the students, every effort would be made to have students who were truly participating members of the school community. It is important to recall that participation means, for Wojtyla, the knowledge that each person is valued for their opinion and contribution and that this opinion and contribution actually finds its way into the overall work of the community. Thus, the old adage that "children should be seen and not heard" is totally at odds with a school founded upon Wojtyla's personalism. Participation by the students does not necessarily mean that everything they "want" is handed over to them; rather, it means that students are heard as persons who really do have something to contribute and that their ideas may very well contribute to the growth of the school community. An active program of student input into the workings of the school would definitely be part of the school.

Flowing from the students being active participants in the development of the school community is the need for them to be active participants in their own learning, since, as Wojtyla pointed out numerous times, learning only occurs when the student consciously makes the decision to take ownership of his or her own personal self-education. Gone would be the mentality of education being the giving of information by the teacher to the student. A classroom in which lecture becomes the sole means of instruction would be at odds with students taking on the responsibility for their own education. Students would need to be assisted in their own pursuit of information; guided by their teachers, students would be the ones who discover the excitement of learning. It is within this process that the students will begin to be awakened to the importance of seeking the truth and acting in accord with the truth once found, in other words, the process of self-education leading to self-fulfillment.

Because there is the need to offer structure to the life of the student, often when it is unwelcome, discipline would be an aspect of the life of the student at Wojtyla's school. This discipline would, however, have to meet the criteria of being in line with respecting the personhood of the student. Thus, any discipline, whether in word or action, must never demean or belittle the student. Discipline, correctly offered, will help the student to see more clearly the manner in which they can align their action with good or true acts.

The Parents. As has been seen, the parental role in education figures very prominently in Wojtyla's overall philosophy of education. For this reason, the parents of the students in Wojtyla's school would continue to play an important part in the education of their children. Since the parents of a child are, by natural right, the first educators of their child, the school's role will be one of assisting them in their role, not supplanting them. Given the current conditions in which many parents find themselves, unable or unwilling to be "parent" for their child, Wojtyla's school must walk the fine line between over and under involvement in the life of the child. Wojtyla has explained that even in the best of circumstances, the school cannot replace the parents and family community, therefore a concerted effort must be made to keep the parents connected to the education of their child, even if this proves to be difficult.

Parents are, as well, the first ones to begin the child's introduction into a community (the community of the family) as well as helping to inaugurate the process of self-education. In Wojtyla's school, parents would be encouraged to become fully participating members of the school community. While this will often mean more effort on the part of all concerned, the good of the child depends upon it, as parents are able to continue the work which they began in the home.

The Faculty. The importance of the faculty in Wojtyla's school being people who understand the need to respect and love their students cannot be understated. Teachers, who are worthy of the title, are those who see their position not as a job to provide an income, but a vocation in which they share in the development of a new generation of human persons.

A faculty with this mindset cannot just be hired, but must be nurtured. They have to perceive themselves as being valued in their personhood by the administrators, students and parents. If the school wishes them to be models of service to the students, the faculty cannot be treated in ways which causes them to feel that they are "merely employees" of the school Here the delicate issue of a just wage must be raised as well. Teachers who do not receive a just wage will not see themselves as being respected in their personhood, for indeed, they are not receiving the respect they deserve. The manner in which requests are made of them or issues raised with them must reflect the value in which their personhood is held by the administration. While this nurturing may often require much sacrifice on the part of the administrator, it is the only way in which the school will be able to provide models of self-fulfilled adults for the students.

Going hand in glove with the respect which needs to be afforded each individual faculty member is the need to have the faculty be participating members of the school community. Just as with the students and parents, the faculty need to know that they are valued for the opinion and the contribution they make to the school. This requires taking the time to listen to what each faculty member has to say and to have them as part of the decision making process. It is only when and where this participation actually comes into existence that a spirit of solidarity will develop; a spirit where each member of the faculty knows themselves to be part of a community moving toward the same goal or goals. Wojtyla's school would again be always working toward this level of solidarity so that it can assist the students in their work of self-education.

Wojtyla's school would also be a place where faculty development is considered the norm and every opportunity for this development would be offered. As Wojtyla noted each time he spoke with Catholic school teachers, the importance of their vocation as models for the young people who attend their schools requires of them that they continue to learn themselves, both for their own self-fulfillment and for the good of their students. This life-long learning on the part of the faculty will also help them to show their students how they continue to search for the truth in their own lives. It is here that students can come to understand that truth is not something which is ever fully possessed by the person, but rather a continual process of searching which goes on all throughout life; self-education never ends. Additionally, there is always the need to familiarize oneself with new pedagogical methods so as to make use of the new findings regarding education.

It has been mentioned above that in order for teachers to be able to effectively carry out their role within the school, they need to be participating member of the school community and share in the spirit of solidarity. Another important aspect of promoting solidarity is that the faculty participate in the development of the vision for Wojtyla's school. This vision, developed with all stake holders in the school community, must be clearly articulated to and by the faculty. Solidarity will only develop properly if the entire community has a shared vision. In Wojtyla's school, the faculty would play an important part in helping the school administrators develop and articulate an appropriate and meaningful vision for the school community.

The School Administrators. The operative word for the school administrators in Wojtyla's school would be service. The administrator's role is to provide the entire community with a model of service by their willingness to be of service to the school community. The administrator who views his or her position as being one of honor or authority would have no place in a school which is based upon Wojtyla's educational philosophy. Service to the school community can take many forms, and, respecting the principle of subsidiarity, no administrator should see a job or duty as beneath him or her.

By the very nature of their positions, administrators can easily be the cause of individual persons being alienated from the school community. This is particularly so in the administrators' interaction with the faculty and parents, where even the tone of one's voice can be enough to cause another not to be treated as their dignity as a person demands. Administrators in Wojtyla's school would be men and women who know how to bring people together in a spirit of solidarity by assisting them to become participating members of the school community as well as formers of the school's vision leading to solidarity. This ability will only be in place if the administrator truly values the personhood of others and knows how to listen to them; rudeness and sarcasm would be entirely out of place in any administrator in Wojtyla's school.

As was mentioned above, all traces of "institutional alienation" must be rooted out and the ones who must lead the battle against this are the administrators. They need to be ever vigilant in reviewing any policy which is put forward for its conformity with the stated vision of the school community as well as whether the policy is in accord with treating all persons as subjects in, and not objects of, the school. It must always be recalled that the school exists for the person, not the person for the school.

Curriculum and Methodology. Given the fact that Wojtyla himself has never put forward a model curriculum, one may take the educated guess that he would accept Religion, English, History, Math, Science, Foreign Language, Fine Arts, and Physical Education as being appropriate for his school, if located in the United States. He would obviously bow to differences of culture which might call for various other subjects to be added as the need arose. The rule of thumb which would, however, need to be followed when designing the curriculum for Wojtyla's school would be each subject being directed to helping the student arrive at the truth so necessary for self-education and self-fulfillment. Therefore, any subject which was interwoven with half-truths or propaganda would be unworthy of the student and should not be taught.

Because of the central place which Jesus Christ holds in Wojtyla's philosophy of education, specifically as a model to follow, the teaching of Religion would be of paramount importance. Wojtyla's school would be a place where the student would be invited to come to know the person of Jesus Christ, not just know various facts about him. Since the goal of all catechesis is the establishment of a true and thereby, personal, relationship with Jesus, the teaching of Religion would not just be the acquiring of intellectual knowledge, but also the experiential dimension of faith. Additionally, because in the person of Jesus it is possible to find truth incarnate, all educators within the school community would need to reference their search for truth to Jesus. Again, the individual consciences of the students would need to be respected here as well.

In Wojtyla's school, the specific content of each course in each subject area would be based upon the judgment of the experts in that particular field. What would, however, be a *sine qua non* is that all the subjects must be taught in an integrated fashion so as not to continue the artificial division of knowledge and truth so prevalent since the Scientific Revolution. Students at Wojtyla's school would continually be reminded, by the example of the faculty in the presentation of their subject, of the unity of all knowledge in the one truth. Any artificial divisions of knowledge which are holdovers from the Modern era would be removed. Students would be helped to realize that education is not the recalling of independent bits of fact, but rather the continual discovery of truth wherever it is found. Also, the concept of responsible stewardship for the world in which humans live would be introduced.

The artificial divisions of knowledge thus removed, Wojtyla's school would also be a place where all knowledge would be presented in a manner which recognizes that students learn when their individual subjectivity is taken into account. It should be recalled that even while holding that all persons are to seek after the truth, Wojtyla reminds his readers of the fact that each person's perception of that truth may be different. These various perceptions of the truth would be taken into account so that, over the course of time, incorrect perceptions may be identified and the search for truth continue. Here again, the role of the teacher will be extremely important: material must be presented in a way which acknowledges the students particular worldview and ability. Each person is different and this difference would be taken into account in Wojtyla's model school.

Because of the importance of personal experience in the process of self-education, the students in Wojtyla's school would be exposed to a diversity of experiences so that they will be better equipped to proceed with their self-education. The school would provide students with new educational experiences so that the personal resources upon which they can draw would be increased. Simply put, the students would be help to see that the world of their youth is not the complete picture of the world of humanity.

In terms of methodology, there would be a need for all educators within the school community to continue to assess the techniques used and the effectiveness of these techniques. Since students are the active forces in their self-education, the teacher must envision new methods in which the students take on an ever increasing independence within the learning process. Educational methodologies such as cooperative learning and independent research would be used along with the tools which computer technology is offering at ever increasing rates. In order to maintain the understanding that education is not just confined to the classroom or the school building, advantage would be taken of learning opportunities in other settings.

While teachers would be anxious to work with each other to provide a holistic vision of learning to the students, there would also be time set aside for the students to be assisted with the process of integrating their new-found knowledge into their personal experience of life. This time would allow the student to think and to sort out how all of this relates to their choice of vocation in life as well as the human acts which they freely choose to perform. It would be hoped that this added dimension will be an avenue of helping the student see in inter-relatedness of their learning, truth, and the choices they make.

In order to help the student move further along the path of understanding that living with other human persons involves the very real project of self-gift, the Wojtyla school would make community service an integral part of the overall program. This service to community should not be seen as one which is "tacked on" to the overall school program, but rather a continual process where students are brought ever more deeply to the realization that their self-fulfillment (the goal of their education) is dependent upon their willingness to give of themselves in service to other human persons. Probably the single most important element here would be that community service not be something limited to students alone. All members of the school community, joined in a spirit of solidarity, would seek to make concrete their self-education by helping to transform the culture in which they live into one fully respectful of all persons. A culture where all human persons can participate and can therefore move toward their own self-fulfillment in response to the truth.

The Wojtyla School in Perspective. There is little doubt that the picture of Wojtyla's model school has been painted with very broad strokes indeed. There can be little doubt as well that even this brief sketch could be open to the charge of being hopelessly utopian and pollyannaish. While both of these charges may well be true, the need to keep this "utopian" model in view is obvious; achieving a perfect embodiment of it may be nearly impossible, but to give up the desire to bring it about would mean that educators have settled for the "good enough" school instead of working for the "what should be" school.

As one reads through the above approaches to the school community, it is clear that many, if not all, of the things mentioned are not new. Indeed, they are many of the things which Catholic school educators have been trying to bring about in their own schools. One need only to read such texts as Thomas Groome's *Educating for Life* to see many of the same ideas presented and Bryk, Lee and Holland's *Catholic Schools and the Common Good* to see the success of many of the same ideas. This being so, what can be said regarding Wojtyla's contribution to a uniquely Catholic philosophy of education?

VIII

WOJTYLA AND
CATHOLIC EDUCATIONAL THOUGHT

This investigation set out on the road to reopen the dialogue necessary to work toward developing a Catholic philosophy of education for the 21st century. A philosophy of education which was both "old" and "new;" one which took from the best of previous Catholic philosophical traditions and one which moved forward by incorporating some of the insights into the human person by 20th century philosophers. It was suggested that Karol Wojtyla's personalism might well help to accomplish this task. Having come to the end of the journey, we are faced with answering whether Wojtyla's thought provides just such a help.

The question asked at the conclusion of the previous section provides a good starting point in trying to assess the value of Wojtyla's work for Catholic educators. Given the fact that, in many cases, the practical application of his thought reflects much of what is already going on in Catholic schools, what can his thought be said to contribute?

In terms of the actual praxis within schools, there is not a significant amount which is new. The area where Wojtyla has contributed is in the fact that he has once again, as he himself says about most of his philosophical writing, brought philosophical theory to the practice which his experiences validated. Wojtyla has indeed provided a philosophy of education which helps Catholic school educators understand *why* what they *do* each day works so well for their students. He has presented a view of the human person which is very much person-centered and based upon individual experiences of self, while maintaining the reality of the existence (*suppositum*) of the person. While experience and consciousness help to form who we are, they are not the cause of our existence. Thus he has taken from both the "old" and the "new." His thought has helped move Catholic educational philosophy toward being more person "centered," by recognizing the need to be conscious of the personal experience of each student. The latest document from the Congregation for Catholic Education, *The Catholic School on the Threshold of the Third Millennium* (1997), although a hortatory document rather than a philosophical one, seems to call for certain approaches in education which can be traced to Wojtyla's thought.

This being said, in no way can Wojtyla's work be looked upon as being *the* philosophy of education which should be adopted by all. Rather, it should be looked upon as a solid source of theory for those educators who continue to see the validity of Thomistic metaphysics. Those who have moved on from St. Thomas to a more postmodern approach to philosophy will not find in Wojtyla's ideas anything of great benefit to them. What could be of most benefit coming from Wojtyla's work would be a renewed interest in understanding the theory behind what we do as educators. It is often the case that, in being so involved in the doing, we forget to ask what it is that makes what we are doing work.

In addition to providing an invitation for Catholic school educators to enter into discussion about the philosophical theory behind their chosen vocation as teachers, it would appear that Wojtyla's work introduces enough phenomenological method into Thomistic metaphysics to provide an opening for a dialogue with Postmodern Catholic educational thinkers. While it may be hoping against hope that any substantive agreement can be generated with the deconstructionist branch of postmodernism, there is every reason to think that dialogue with the more moderate, or constructionist, postmodern thinkers could arrive at substantive agreement to the benefit of the work of Catholic education as we move into the 21st century.

In any case, it should be recalled that Wojtyla's philosophical work remains incomplete because of his change in roles from philosopher to authoritative teacher. As Buttiglione (1993) states, "It [Wojtyla's philosophical thought] indicates paths, delineates hypotheses for research, begins a deep investigation, and shows new horizons. It thereby requires to be taken forward" (p. 306). It is hoped that this investigation has moved Wojtyla's philosophical work forward by drawing forth from his papal writings the kernels of his philosophical thought which will contribute to the continual unfolding of a Catholic philosophy of education for the 21st century.

While progressing through this research into Karol Wojtyla's thought, a number of areas presented themselves as both interesting and important ideas or concepts to be delved into at greater length.

The first area was hinted at above: the work of entering into dialogue, on a philosophical level, with the constructionist postmodern thinkers, both within Catholic circles and in the public sector. The questions to be raised are manifold, particularly when one asks whether Wojtyla's educational philosophy can really ever be separated from Catholicism. However, the benefits of the approach which Wojtyla takes toward the human person, especially considering the sound educational results which come about when it is followed, would be a good starting point for dialogue, especially with non-Catholic Christians and public school educators. In *Educating for Life,* Thomas Groome (1998) asks much the same question: does Catholic educational practice really need to be so sectarian (pp. 53-56)?

The next question is much more philosophical. It deals with Wojtyla's emphasis on the *communio personarum.* Given the intimate nature of the *communio personarum*, especially as described in reference to the family, can a large school or university really claim to be able to form a *communio personarum* which would enable the processes of horizontal transcendence, self-education, and self-fulfillment to go on as Wojtyla describes them? And if these schools, by their size, are not really capable of establishing a true *communio personarum*, how can their effectiveness be explained? Either the *communio personarum* does come into existence in some, up to now, unrecognizable form or the establishment of a *communio personarum* is not as intrinsic to education as Wojtyla maintains. Which ever may be the case, the issue deserves further investigation.

The final question which comes to the fore is whether it is really ever possible to come to an equitable solution to the conflict between academic freedom and the magisterial and/or infallible teaching of the Catholic Church. When, in a Catholic university, theologians seek to debate the validity of truths which have been defined as revealed truths by the Church's Magisterium, do they have a right to do so because of academic freedom? *Ex Corde Ecclesiae* has provided an opening for this discussion, but there are many facets to this discussion which need to be addressed. Flowing from this debate is the question as to whether Wojtyla (or any pope, for that matter) can be engaged in an academic, philosophical discussion concerning this issue. Is it possible to be the philosopher and the authoritative teacher at the same time and openly engage in academic dialogue? While this issue is one which necessitates investigation regarding ecclesiology as well as education and the school, it certainly does warrant further study and dialogue.

Discussion in any of these areas will, it seems, bring Catholic educators to the important task of formulating a Catholic philosophy of education. John Paul II's ideas are a beginning: it is the collective experience of those who teach each day which will bring the work to yet greater fulfillment.

REFERENCES

Ashley, B. (1996). *Justice in the Church: Gender and participation.* Washington, DC: The Catholic University of America Press.

Barzun, J., & Graff, H. (1992). *The modern researcher.* Boston: Houghton Mifflin Company.

Bloch, A., & Czuczka, G. (Eds.). (1981). *Toward a philosophy of praxis.* New York: Crossroad Publishing Company.

Bryk, A., Lee, V., & Holland, P. (1993). *Catholic schools and the common good.* Cambridge, MA: Harvard University Press.

Buber, M. (1996). *I and thou.* New York: Touchstone.

Buetow, H. (1988). *The Catholic school.* New York: Crossroad Publishing Company.

Buttiglione, R. (1997). *Karol Wojtyla: The thought of the man who became Pope John Paul II.* Grand Rapids, MI: William B. Eerdmans Publishing Company.

Cahill, L. (1994). Accent on the masculine. In J. Wilkins (Ed.), *Considering Veritatis Splendor* (pp. 53-60). Cleveland, OH: The Pilgrim Press.

Caldecott, S. (1992). Towards a distinctively Catholic school. *Communio,* 19(2), 271-277.

Congregation for Catholic Education. (1977). The Catholic school. [CD-ROM]. *Catholic Desktop Library.* Boston: Pauline Software.

Congregation for Catholic Education. (1988). The religious dimension of education in a Catholic school. [CD-ROM]. *Catholic Desktop Library.* Boston: Pauline Software.

Congregation for Catholic Education. (1997). The Catholic school on the threshold of the third millenium. [CD-ROM]. *Catholic Desktop Library.* Boston: Pauline Software.

Daw, R. (Ed.). (1987). *Pope John Paul II: Building up the body of Christ.* San Francisco: Ignatius Press.

Doran, K. (1996). *Solidarity: A synthesis of personalism and communalism in the thought of Karol Wojtyla.* New York: Peter Lang.

Elias, J. (1997). *Catholic educational theory in the 19th and 20th centuries.* Unpublished manuscript.

Elias, J. (1999). Whatever happened to Catholic philosophy of education? *Religious Education,* 94 (1), 92-110.

Frossard, A. (1984). *Be not afraid.* New York: St. Martin's Press.

Gleason, P. (1995). *Contending with modernity.* New York: Oxford University Press.

Grondelski, J. (1993). Sources for the study of Karol Wojtyla's thought. In K. Schmitz, *At the center of the human drama: The philosophical anthropology of Karol Wojtyla* (pp. 147-163). Washington, DC: The Catholic University of America Press.

Groome, T. (1998). *Educating for life.* Allen, TX: Thomas More Press.

Haring, B. (1994). A distrust that wounds. In J. Wilkins (Ed.), *Considering Veritatis Splendor* (pp. 9-13). Cleveland, OH: The Pilgrim Press.

Hellman, J. (1981). *Emmanuel Mounier and the new Catholic Left: 1930-1950.* Toronto, Canada: University of Toronto Press.

Jencks, C. (1986). *What is post-modernism?* New York: St. Martin's Press.

Komonchak, J. (1993). The Catholic university in the Church. In J. Langan (Ed.), *Catholic universities in Church and society: A dialogue on Ex Corde Ecclesiae* (pp. 35-55). Washington, DC: Georgetown University Press.

Kwitny, J. (1997). *Man of the century: The life and times of Pope John Paul II.* New York: Henry Holt and Company.

Langan, J. (Ed.). (1993). *Catholic universities in Church and society: A dialogue on Ex Corde Ecclesiae.* Washington, DC: Georgetown University Press.

Lorsung, T. (Ed.). (1993). *John Paul II speaks to youth.* San Francisco: Ignatius Press.

Lyotard, J. (1993). *The postmodern explained.* Minneapolis, MN: University of Minnesota Press.

Malinski, M. (1979). *Pope John Paul II: The life of Karol Wojtyla.* New York: Seabury.

Maritain, J. (1943). *Education at the crossroads.* New Haven, CT: Yale University Press.

McLean, G. (1994). Preface. In J. Tischner, J. Zycinski, & G. McLean (Eds.), *The philosophy of person: Solidarity and cultural creativity* (pp. vii-x). Washington, DC: The Council for Research in Values and Philosophy.

Mounier, E. (1970). *Personalism.* Notre Dame, IN: University of Notre Dame Press.

Noddings, N. (1992). *The challenge to care in schools.* New York: Teachers College Press.

Novak, M. (1997). John Paul II: Christian philosopher. *America,* 177(12), 11-16.

O'Brien, D. (1998). *The hidden pope.* New York: Daybreak Books.

Pius XI. (1929). Divini Illius Magistri. [CD-ROM]. *Catholic Desktop Library.* Boston: Pauline Software.

Schmitz, K. (1989). From anarchy to principles: Deconstruction and the resources of Christian philosophy. *Communio,* 16(1), 69-88.

Schmitz, K. (1993). *At the center of the human drama: The philosophical anthropology of Karol Wojtyla.* Washington, D.C.: The Catholic University of America Press.

Seifert, J. (1981). Karol Cardinal Wojtyla as philosopher and the Cracow/Lublin school of philosophy. [On-line]. Available: www.iap.li/html/aletheia_ii.html

Slattery, P. (1995). *Curriculum development in the postmodern era.* New York: Garland Publishing.

Taborski, B. (1987). Introduction. In K. Wojtyla, *The collected plays and writings on theater* (pp. 1-16). Berkeley, CA: University of California Press.

Taylor, M. (1986). *Deconstruction in context: Literature and philosophy.* Chicago: The University of Chicago Press.

Tischner, J., Zycinski, J., & McLean, G. (Eds.). (1994). *The philosophy of person: Solidarity and cultural creativity.* Washington, DC: The Council for Research in Values and Philosophy.

Weigel, G. (1999). *Witness to hope.* New York: HarperCollins Publishers.

Wilkins, J. (Ed.). (1994). *Considering Veritatis Splendor.* Cleveland, OH: The Pilgrim Press.

Wojtyla, K. (1959). *On the possibility of constructing a Christian ethic on the basis of the system of Max Scheler.* Lublin, Poland: Towarzystwo Naukowe KUL.

Wojtyla, K. (1979a). *The acting person.* Boston: D. Reidel Publishing Company.

Wojtyla, K/John Paul II. (1979b). Catechesi Tradendae. [CD-ROM]. *Catholic Desktop Library.* Boston: Pauline Software.

Wojtyla, K/John Paul II. (1979c). Redemptor Hominis. [CD-ROM]. *Catholic Desktop Library.* Boston: Pauline Software.

Wojtyla, K/John Paul II. (1979d). Address to European journalists and members of the Italian commission for the international year of the child, 13 January 1979. In A. Bloch & G. Czuczka (Eds.), *Toward a philosophy of praxis* (pp. 128-129). New York: Crossroad Publishing Company.

Wojtyla, K. (1980a). *Sources of renewal: The implementation of the Second Vatican Council.* San Francisco: Harper and Row.

Wojtyla, K. (1980b). *The jeweler's shop.* San Francisco: Ignatius Press.

Wojtyla, K/John Paul II. (1981a). Familiaris Consortio. [CD-ROM]. *Catholic Desktop Library.* Boston: Pauline Software.

Wojtyla, K. (1981b). *Love and responsibility.* San Francisco: Ignatius Press.

Wojtyla, K/John Paul II. (1981c). Laborem Exercens. [On-line]. Available: http://www.vatican.va/holy_father/john_paul_ii/encyclicals/documents/hf_jp-ii_enc_14091981_laborem-exercens_en.html

Wojtyla, K. (1981d). *Faith according to St. John of the Cross.* San Francisco: Ignatius Press.

Wojtyla, K. (1982). *Persona y accion* [Person and act]. Madrid: Biblioteca de Autores Cristianos.

Wojtyla, K/John Paul II. (1985). To the youth of the world. [CD-ROM]. *Catholic Desktop Library.* Boston: Pauline Software.

Wojtyla, K. (1987a). *The collected plays and writings on theater.* Berkeley, CA: University of California Press.

Wojtyla, K/John Paul II. (1987b). Address to Catholic school teachers, New Orleans, 12 September 1987. In R. Daw (Ed.), *Pope John Paul II: Building up the body of Christ* (pp. 152-155). San Francisco: Ignatius Press.

Wojtyla, K/John Paul II. (1987c). Address to university professors, New Orleans, 12 September 1987. In R. Daw (Ed.), *Pope John Paul II: Building up the body of Christ* (pp. 160-163). San Francisco: Ignatius Press.

Wojtyla, K/John Paul II. (1990a). Ex Corde Ecclesiae [CD-ROM]. *Catholic Desktop Library.* Boston: Pauline Software.

Wojtyla, K/John Paul II. (1990b). Message for the VI world youth day. [On-line]. Available: http://www.vatican.va/holy_father/john_paul_ii/

messages/youth/documents/hf_jp-ii_mes_15081990_vi-world-youth-day_en.html

Wojtyla, K./John Paul II. (1991). Message for the VII world youth day. [On-line]. Available: http://www.vatican.va/holy_father/john_paul_ii/messages/youth/documents/hf_jp-ii_mes_24111991_vii-world-youth-day_en.html

Wojtyla, K./John Paul II. (1992). Message for the VIII world youth day. [On-line]. Available: http://www.vatican.va/holy_father/john_paul_ii/messages/youth/documents/hf_jp-ii_mes_15081992_viii-world-youth-day_en.html

Wojtyla, K. (1993). *Person and community: Selected essays.* New York: Peter Lang.

Wojtyla, K./John Paul II. (1994a). Veritatis Splendor. [On-line]. Available: http://www.vatican.va/holy_father/phf_en.htm

Wojtyla, K./John Paul II. (1994b). Letter to families. [CD-ROM]. *Catholic Desktop Library.* Boston: Pauline Software.

Wojtyla, K./John Paul II. (1994c). *Crossing the threshold of hope.* New York: Knopf.

Wojtyla, K./John Paul II. (1995a). Homily at Central Park, NY, October 7. [On-line]. Available: http://www.ewtn.com/library/PAPALDOC/JP2US95H.HTM

Wojtyla, K./John Paul II. (1995b). Message for the XI world youth day. [On-line]. Available: http://www.vatican.va/holy_father/john_paul_ii/messages/youth/documents/hf_jp-ii_mes_26111995_xi-world-youth-day_en.html

Wojtyla, K./John Paul II. (1996). Message for the XII world youth day. [On-line]. Available: http://www.vatican.va/holy_father/john_paul_ii/messages/youth/documents/hf_jp-ii_mes_15081996_xii-world-youth-day_en.html

Wojtyla, K. (1997a). *The place within: The poetry of pope John Paul II.* New York: Random House.

Wojtyla, K./John Paul II. (1997b). Address to the Villa Flaminia Institute. [On-line]. Available: http://www.ewtn.com/library/PAPALDOC/JP97223.TXT

Wojtyla, K./John Paul II. (1997c). Address to the rectors of Polish universities. [On-line]. Available: http://www.vatican.va/news_service/or/viag_ap/pold_eng.html

Wojtyla, K/John Paul II. (1997d). Address to youth in Poznan, Poland. [On-line]. Available: http://www.vatican.va/holy_father/john_paul_ii/travels/documents/hf_jp-ii_spe_03061997_youth_en.html

Wojtyla, K/John Paul II. (1997e). Message for the XIII world youth day. [On-line]. Available: http://www.vatican.va/holy_father/john_paul_ii/messages/youth/documents/hf_jp-ii_mes_30111997_xiii-world-youth-day_en.html

Wojtyla, K/John Paul II. (1998a). Fides et Ratio. [On-line]. Available: http://www.vatican.va/holy_father/phf_en.htm

Wojtyla, K/John Paul II. (1998b). Message to the young people of Cuba. [On-line]. Available: http://www.vatican.va/holy_father/john_paul_ii/travels/documents/hf_jp-ii_mes_23011998_lahavana-youth_en.html

Wojtyla, K/John Paul II. (1999). Address to the young people of St. Louis. [On-line]. Available: http://www.vatican.va/holy_father/john_paul_ii/travels/documents/hf_jp-ii_spe_26011999_stlouis-youth_en.html

INDEX